My '70s
Book

The "When I Was A Kid…" Book
For The Generation That Grew Up In The '70s

Darryll Sherman

First published by Dog Ear Publishing
4010 W. 86th Street, Ste H
Indianapolis, IN 46268
www.dogearpublishing.net

ISBN: 978-159858-690-9

This book is printed on acid-free paper.

Printed in the United States of America

Acknowledgements:

I would like to express my sincerest thanks to the following people:

To my wife and kids, who totally supported me throughout this whole crazy book-writing escapade. Their love, dedication, and encouragement were instrumental in my completing the project.

To my Mom and Dad, who successfully raised my siblings and me through the '70s (well, through all the decades of our lives, I guess) and contributed to my lifetime of memories with love, care, guidance, and overall family fun and adventure.

To my sisters, Leanne and Gayle, who were a constant source of information and support.

To my brother, Keith, who has been my best friend and was the other half of almost all of my memories growing up. He has the uncanny ability to remember everything all of us ever did at any/every family event. His help has been invaluable and greatly appreciated.

To all of my friends, who lived life with me growing up. You are a significant part of why I wrote this book; those whose names I don't recall as well as those who are close friends of mine still today.

To the friends who took the time to read my work in its infancy and willingly offered their help and advice throughout the process. Your little ideas sometimes made big differences.

To all of you who endured my endless questions for ideas and clarifications of our memories together and individually – I couldn't have done it without you!

To Nancy Mace - a special thanks for her incredible editing work and for her professional and personal encouragement of my attempt at writing.

To Cheryl Mitchell, for her excellent illustrations.

Dedication

To my Mom, who was an amazing example of unselfish love to me and our family.

Contents

Preface

PREFACE

OK – so this is what happened. Awhile back, I noticed how many times my friends and I kept talking about how things were different when we were kids. I know, I know – this is something that we all grew up with…our parents said this to us all the time. We've all heard the stories of how they trudged uphill through endless snow drifts, barefoot, to and from school; how they can remember the very first TVs they ever saw; how they all made do with a lot less than we have today. So – like most of us – I grew up thinking that they didn't know what they were talking about, and then – like most of us – I eventually became a parent and caught myself saying the same sorts of things to my kid and her friends.

Gradually I realized that I could recall a lot of experiences that – I thought – were different when *I* was a kid. Like, how we were lucky to get one "big" gift at Christmas (which we often had to share with our brother or sister); or, how we had to actually do chores – *real* chores – to earn our allowance… and if we didn't do them, we didn't get our allowance; and how whining never got us anything but a well-deserved swat on the rear end.

A lot of the things that kids have today - the toys, the endless options for entertainment, the door-to-door service from their soccer moms – are all so much more than I ever had growing up. But I've also realized that I had a lot of things that they don't have: like the *need* for pretending, imagining or make-believe; I had the ability to carry on an intelligent conversation without interjecting multiple "likes" and "ums" and "you knows;" and I was able to pay attention to something for more than 5 minutes without it having to be extremely entertaining.

About the same time I was having these realizations, there seemed to be a rebirth of everything from the '70s. Whether it was music, hair, clothes, cars, styles, fashions, home decor... it seemed that I was seeing things from my past everywhere I turned. This just reinforced the idea that I had to start writing down all these thoughts. So, my thoughts turned into a little pile of notes and scribbles, and, well, then this book just kind of happened. I've found that I tend to write like I think. Be that good or bad, I hope that it's entertaining to you and helps you relive some of your fond childhood memories, too.

This book is my observations about how my life was when and where I grew up. Now, I know that we all lived different lives. There's a good chance that this won't be an accurate reflection of your childhood years if you grew up in a richy-rich neighborhood, or if you grew up in the inner city of some metropolis. But, for the many of us who grew up in suburbia, Anytown, USA, my babbling may bring back some memories you can relate to – hopefully all good. By the way – I was a pretty good kid and didn't get into too much trouble, for which I thank my parents! I wasn't an angel, but you won't be reading about how my friends and I got drunk and lit a string of firecrackers tied to the cat's tail, or anything like that.

So – sit back, kick off your shoes, grab a grande mocha at Starbucks (now that, folks, is how you execute a shameless plug) and allow yourself to take the time to enjoy the memories of a simpler life.

Chapter 1
How Did I Get to Be 48?

I mean really…how did this happen?

It didn't really sneak up on me…I mean, of course I knew that it was coming… this "getting old(er)" thing. But I think what I wasn't expecting was that I would actually *realize* that I wasn't young anymore. It's easy to continually think that you're still young, or at least younger than you really are, especially when you do a lot of things in life that help you feel like you're still young.

It seems like there ought to be some "exclusion" rules. You know – if I don't have or do certain things… or if I *still* have or do certain things, then – by definition – I'm not *really* old, right? For example – if I don't even have a will, or if I don't set up a responsible retirement plan – then I'm not really old, am I? Or – if I still have all of my old Hot Wheels, or I still spend an occasional Saturday morning watching cartoons… well… *then* I'm not really old, am I? I think I'm grasping at straws here.

I'm fortunate enough to not have any health problems, still have all my hair, and I don't need glasses. I've been involved in a group that interacts with lots of college students on a frequent basis. I also play racquetball pretty regularly and am fairly active overall. I still *feel* young!

But... it's becoming more and more evident that I am indeed aging, and that my generation is no longer the young and hip generation (I know, I'm something like two generations off the lead now). I remember that I used to think 30 was old... and then I thought 40 was old... pretty soon 50 won't be old. Or – 50 will be the new 40... just like 40 was the new 30... well, you get the idea.

I really have to just take a step back and face the fact... I am almost 50! Can this really be possible? There must be some sort of mistake! Sometimes, my brother and sisters and I all sit around and discuss our ages in disbelief. We still call ourselves "the kids," our folks' name for us. We've all got good jobs, families, 2.5 kids... and even some of them are married. But – we still feel like kids! And my brother and I especially still act like kids, too.

I guess that I could quote the Monday morning water cooler back-and-forth regarding the fact that I'm getting older and say "Well, it beats the alternative!"

And, obviously, I do agree that I'd rather be 48 than... well... the alternative.

So, as I've pondered, reflected, fretted, and maybe even regretted getting older, I've come to a conclusion: I have a lifetime of memories – or at least 40 some-odd years worth – and I wouldn't trade them for anything. That's not to say that I've enjoyed every minute of every day of every year. There are plenty of unpleasant memories that have transpired over the years – the loss of friends and loved ones, financial woes, relational disappointments – but it's all been a part of my life and has made me who and what I am.

If you're right around the same age as I am, I'm sure you can relate. I'm sure that sometimes you have that heart-skipping-a-beat feeling when you realize that there's a good chance that – by the odds – your life is more than half over. Yeah – sorry about that. Well, the intent of my recollections, musings, and perhaps humorous observations, is not to cause you to fret over this, but rather to help you recall your own childhood experiences, maybe cause you to reflect on what it is in your childhood that shaped and molded you to be uniquely you, and last but not least – maybe give you a chance to look back and have a few laughs.

Chapter 2

Playing Was Different When I Was a Kid

"Can we go outside and play?"

These words were the anthem of our summers, and what playing we did! We didn't have Gameboys, or any other hand-held video games, or remote-controlled miniature hummers that cost more than we ever got for a whole summer of picking dandelions, salting slugs, and otherwise earning allowances. We had dirt... and sticks... and trees... maybe even a few scraps of wood fashioned into a machine gun... and... we had vacant lots in which to play.

These vacant lots housed every semi-organized game that we could think of... softball, soccer, football, red light/green light, kickball. We climbed trees, ate green (as in not-ripe-yet) apples, ate plenty of pears and cherries, and explored and created. With our minds at the age of heightened imagination, these vacant lots often became our make-believe worlds. Blackberry bushes were plentiful in our area, and to us they became jungles where we built finely-crafted trails and carved out secret meeting places. We would spend hours using sticks to hack our way through all of the blackberry vines and then haul them out. It never occurred to us that we were working hard because we were having so much fun doing it while making our camps. We could be in as many different places around the neighborhood as there were kids out playing that day, and with our "secret calls" we knew to all jump on our bikes and make for the camp in the bushes – making sure we weren't being followed by any of the "uncool" kids – so we could get together and make plans for the next spurt of fun.

Camps:

Camps were an integral part of our lives growing up. We didn't have the liberty to go hang out at malls, nor did we really want to; there weren't nearly as many shops that appealed to teens as there are today. A camp could take on many different sizes and shapes. A bunch of blankets draped over the couches in the living room; some old sheets of plywood leaning or even nailed together in the corner of someone's back yard; a clearing in a big patch of blackberry bushes with a main tunnel entrance – and, of course, an escape tunnel for quick getaways.

But the ultimate camp was a treecamp. There was nothing that compared when it came to the fun that could be had surrounding treecamps. The idea would come on an otherwise typical summer's day – after we had spent a few days prior engaged in various other activities, someone would pipe up and say, "Hey – let's make a camp." This would be met with a variety of responses... some enthusiastic, some ho-hums... but then someone would say, "How about a *tree*camp?" And suddenly our ears would perk up and we'd start taking the thought seriously.

We would start our planning right away – we would have to find the perfect tree and get permission to build in it. This wasn't usually very hard. Since there were plenty of trees in our neighborhood – and just about all of our parents would approve of anything that would keep us kids busy and out of their hair for awhile – we usually would be granted access to some deciduous beauty, the tree of choice because of its openness as opposed to the evergreen variety. Little did that tree know that it was about to be swarmed by a whole crew of kids with visions of Swiss Family Robinson dancing in their heads.

Now – I've seen some pretty impressive treecamps in my day, but what I find to be almost unbelievable is that you can now buy kits to build treecamps – or – treehouses, as they are referred to on the Internet. I can think of nothing that would do more to squelch the creativity of adventurous young minds than to have a "tree house kit" to assemble in your backyard tree. I'm willing to bet that the instructions also include all of the latest safety tips and recommendations for the "safe construction of your new treehouse!" There's something to be said for the life-lessons learned through trial and error as a bunch of kids build a treecamp out of whatever they can find, borrow, or scrape up. A few bumps and bruises due to some wood or branch strength miscalculations; some sore thumbs due to a few errant hammer swings; some disappointments and re-designing for the lack of materials… these sorts of things helped mold us all into kids who could improvise, cope, and re-evaluate when problems arose. You know – the same type of things that we all run into all the time in our everyday adult lives. The kids who build a treehouse kit today may learn some assembly skills, and how to follow directions, but I think they miss out on the more important qualities that I know I learned as a kid trying to build a treecamp without a plan and using whatever materials we could find. And I'm not against being safe, but I know that in the couple times that I tumbled out of a tree during construction, or fell off a few branches while being stupid and reaching farther than I should have, I learned a lot more than if I had just read, "It is highly recommended that you wear your safety goggles when performing any construction work" in some treehouse construction manual.

Once we had selected a tree, we had to start our "material acquisition phase" (that's fancy talk for "find stuff to build it with"). New house construction was our primary target for these endeavors. If we knew of a new house being built, we were not beyond riding our bikes a considerable distance for the riches to be found there. If I were to recommend this in today's world, I would be yelled at by every parent who would say I'm crazy for thinking that we can trust our kids like that, and I would get shot at with a pneumatic nail gun by every contractor who is in the habit of setting up surveillance at their job sites to prevent the theft common today... but this is what we did when I was a kid. We would typically arrive at a site after the builders had left for the day and would begin our hunting. We would scrounge every nook and cranny to find all the nails that were dropped by the carpenters. We would have never considered taking nails out of boxes – which were often left there. We would even take some of the bent ones and use a hammer to pound them out straight on the sidewalk. We also would only take what we were pretty sure was scrap wood. Again – there was usually plenty of new wood just sitting around, but the scrap pile was our lumberyard, and we made the best use of as much wood as we could haul back.

Armed with the spoils of the local construction sites, whatever scraps we could successfully talk our dads out of, and a few hammers and handsaws, we were ready to begin the design and construction of our treecamps. Again – the kids of today, with their "treehouse kits" simply follow a plan... door here, window there, safety rope here, padded cushions there... what do you learn from that? We had to imagine... imagine something that wasn't there yet, and then we had to improvise, guess, do some trial and error, and try to make it work. We made all types of different treecamps – everything from little single platforms to 3 and 4 "room" designs with carpeting (mismatched carpet scraps) and electricity (extension cords and light bulbs).

What a blast it was to spend our days building and playing in these things – and on the rare nights that our folks would let us – spend the night in them. I know that this was one of the many things I enjoyed as a kid that was instrumental in shaping who I was. I grew up with a respect for nature, a better understanding of physics (much better than if I'd been taught, I think) and the ability to work with others in a team effort.

Bikes:

I mentioned bike riding. A staple of my life as a kid was riding bikes. It was our escape, our chance for exploring, and our only real mode of transportation. We didn't grow up with soccer moms and their comfortable, convenient mini-vans willing to ferry around the entire neighborhood at the drop of a hat. Some of our families only had one car, and if there was a car available, it was usually a station wagon with no AC, no power anything, and a mom who wasn't going to drive anywhere because she expected us to ride our bikes... that's why they bought them for us.

Of course – we all had stingrays. There was no such thing as a BMX or mountain bike back then. We had the banana seats, the redline slicks, the sissy bars. We popped wheelies and had skidding, jumping, and racing contests. And I'll tell you what, we were cool! We rode our bikes to get everywhere around the neighborhood. We had regular routes we cruised, doing our best to look cool and nonchalant in front of any other kids we saw. We'd do the playing-cards-in-the-spokes thing, and we'd even modify our bikes a bit (double forks, bigger sissy bars, etc.). A few of the vacant lots around were ideal for doing jumps and racing. Our bikes were to us what cell phones are to the kids of today... we hardly went anywhere without them. You felt left out if you didn't have yours when everyone else had theirs. They were also a "place" to hang out... whether it was in a vacant lot, in someone's driveway or on the sidewalk down by the corner store – you could sit around on them, lean against them, or even lie down, drink a coke, and use the seat as a headrest.

We often planned out a whole day around an extensive bike ride. I lived outside the Seattle area near Puget Sound. We'd leave mid-morning and not be home until just around dinner. Our bike rides would often include taking a lunch with us and spending the day going to a bunch of fun places: visiting the horses in some local pastures, spending some great time at the local park throwing a Frisbee, playing on the beach for a while, maybe even splurging and getting a scoop of ice cream at Baskin-Robbins. And we got to each and every place we were going on our bikes. We probably rode between 10 and 15 miles on those days – all the while enjoying the outdoors and having fun. It was cool that I grew up in a time when the world was safe enough that we were able to do this. We'd usually have four to six kids ranging in age from 8 to 16. The only real concern that our parents ever expressed was that we be careful.

I mentioned that all we had were stingrays. These were single speed bikes, not 3-speed, 5-speed, 10-speed, etc. They were hard to pedal up hills, and they weren't really "finely" built. They coasted down hills, but not at any breakneck speeds –we could only pedal a single speed bike so fast. And, when we were kids, there was no such thing as a bike helmet. Now, these are something that I am definitely in favor of – there's no denying the lives they save and severe injuries they prevent. It's just that when we were kids, half of the fun of riding bikes was the wind rushing though our long hair as we coasted down some huge hill, with no hands, of course!

I now own a 21-speed mountain bike that – I think –weighs less than just one of the wheels of my old stingray! I wear a helmet as I bike to and from work every now and then (not as often as I should) and every time I do, I am reminded of the days of my youth and all the fun we would have on our lazy summer day bike rides.

Squirt Gun Fights:

One thing that really blows me away is the "squirt guns" that the kids have today. There are guns that are almost as big as the kids who are struggling to drag them around and shoulder the 5 gallons of water that these behemoths store. When you pull the trigger on these things, you're instantly shooting a continuous stream of water seemingly over 50 feet. Some of them need to be pumped up every now and then, but others are battery powered and will just shoot on demand. There are even some of these squirt guns that look like Glocks or AK-47s.

I remember when I was a kid; there were very few squirt gun options. There were maybe three or four different sizes of a standard handgun-looking squirt gun, and there was a pretty cool one that fit into the grasp of your hand and was almost like a set of brass knuckles. These did not shoot far at all, but the harder you squeezed the trigger, the farther they shot. Of course, this was also a basic design flaw in that the harder you pulled on the trigger, the sooner the cheap plastic would wear out and break. The other basic design flaw that all of these guns had was that in order to get the water into them, you had to pull out that little plastic plug in the back, leaving the plastic T-shaped end in. And, of course, those little plastic things would eventually get bent, not stay in, fall out, and then you would lose them… and then the squirt gun was useless. No matter your best efforts, the water would just drain out the back.

There was one tool in our arsenal of water weapons that was really awesome… and you had to be keeping an eye on things in the house to be the lucky kid who got this. There was little that any of your friends could do to defend against the "squirt bottle." This was nothing more than an empty plastic dishwashing liquid bottle. But, get one of these filled up and not only did you have a pretty good amount of water to work with, but the squeezing action could really force a great stream of water a pretty good distance. And, half of what made for a great summer squirt gun fight was being the one who thought first to either grab a hose or a pre-planned bucket of water for the total drenching effect. Nothing like getting someone with a really a good dousing to be able to say you won the squirt gun fight.

Whether it was a squirt gun fight, spending time running through the sprinkler, or being lucky enough to have a "water wiggle" or know someone who did, cooling off in the summer was always a lot of fun.

War:

Another gun game we played was "war." That's what we called it! This really wasn't too complicated. Get a bunch of kids together, grab your favorite toy gun, find a place to play, choose sides, and start shooting. Here are the simple elements better defined:

Bunch of kids: anywhere from 4 to 12 kids… guys only (duh!), and don't bring your snotty little brother who's just going to cry and want to go home halfway through the fight.

Grab your favorite toy gun: usually homemade – scraps of wood nailed and glued together with a nail head for a sight, we used a handsaw to carve the grip cross-hatching, maybe put black electrical tape on it to make it look cool. Or maybe it was a black plastic toy, but all sound was made by us and our lips – no loud, fancy electronics back then.

Find a place to play: any big, wooded area would do, or even just around the neighborhood, but the boundaries needed to be clearly defined. We also had a great park on the beach on Puget Sound that was hilly and just like the beaches in the movies.

Choose sides: oldest kids got to be team captains by default, take turns choosing sides; last choice was either the smallest or slowest kid.

...and start shooting: and this was what it was all about. There were clear rules about how long you had to stay down when you got shot... count to 50 by ones, or something like that. And once you shot someone, you had to leave the area – you couldn't just wait around and shoot them again. We would play this for hours. There wasn't really a winner, we all followed the rules, and we had fun! It all took a lot of imagination, but in our minds we were engaged in the big conflicts and doing battle with the enemy just like in all the war movies we watched growing up. I'm sure these days that kids would be discouraged from playing "war." Instead, I would guess that a rousing game of "Find the local wetland" or a "Mother Earth Appreciation Walk" would be on the agenda. Although, true to their form, most of the little boys would probably end up grabbing sticks and shooting at each other anyway, much to the chagrin of their "afternoon encouragement counselor."

Yard Games:

I was recently reminiscing with my brother about some of the outdoor games we used to play as kids. We agreed that one of our favorites was "Kick the Can." If you don't know the game, the rules are pretty simple. One person is "it," and everyone else goes and hides. The person who is "it" has to guard a can which was usually just an old coffee can. If he spots someone, say, behind a tree, he and the person he found race for the can. If the person who has been found kicks the can first, he is "free" and everyone else who has already been caught is also "free." But if the person who is "it" jumps over the can first, he "catches" that person.

First, we had to determine who was "it." This was done in a very democratic and universally-accepted fashion. We would employ one of the following methods. First, we would all start yelling "Not It!" at the top of our lungs, and the last person to be heard was "it." This usually didn't work, as it's hard to determine who yelled what when/last/etc. Consequently, we would go to the next step in which we would use one of a variety of elimination techniques to single out a "loser," or the person who was "it." These included "One Potato, Two Potato…," "Eenie Meenie Miney Moe…," "Engine Engine Number Nine…" and probably some others I can't remember.

Of course, the *best* thing was playing this late at night. We'd usually have somewhere between 8 and 20 kids playing. It was awesome to be the "hero" – the last one hiding who then kicks the can and sets everyone free. There was nothing like the feeling of your heart about to beat out of your chest while you held your breath as the person who was "it" walked by… and then, the race to the can was on! What fun; what simple fun it was!

As a family we also played croquet. My dad took special delight in laying out the course and putting wickets on the *top* of little hills in our yard. Half of his fun in playing the game was watching us try to even get our shots to the wickets! And, of course, knocking us out of shooting range whenever he could.

The other fun game we loved to play was Jarts! Man – talk about an accident waiting to happen! In this day and age of ultra-hyper sensitivity about whether anything and everything you buy is safe or not, these things would *never* make it in today's market. I would love to see the TV commercials for these now: a video clip of a happy little family hurling these steel-tipped winged devices at little plastic rings at either end of the front yard. "Make sure to pay attention when the other side is throwing." I wonder how many families ended up in the emergency room with an inadvertently pierced toe or worse. Fortunately, we escaped any such injuries, but we did play it a lot... probably still have the set in my folks' attic! Maybe I should see what I can get for it on eBay.

The concept of "playing" certainly was different when I was a kid, but I wouldn't have wanted it any other way, and I wouldn't trade it for anything the world offers today. Every experience, every mistake, every injury, and every success – all a part of what made me who and what I am.

Chapter 3

Things We DIDN'T Have

Water in a Bottle:

Water bottles. When I was a kid, if you had said this to me, I would have pictured a baby bottle with water in it. Everyone would have. There were no such things as water bottles, bottled water, or *buying* water. Even the *thought* of buying water would have made us laugh out loud. Perhaps some very forward-thinking guy might have envisioned it – but in our minds, it would have only been in a futuristic soci- ety that had depleted the natural resources and *needed* to buy water to survive... not just because you wanted a drink of water. When you wanted a drink of water, you got it from the tap, or a water fountain, or a pitcher at a restaurant, or the hose in the front yard... no one – and especially kids – would ever *think* of walking around with a bottle of water. We only had glass bottles; plastic wasn't used nearly as much as it is today. Recently, there was a commercial on TV showing a bunch of hikers up in the mountains in the '70s (you could tell by the short jean cutoffs and over-the-calf double color striped athletic socks – yeah, remember? You couldn't *buy* jean shorts, you made your jeans into cutoffs when the holes in the knees got too big. And they were short... like almost *indecently* short... not the knee-length ones you buy today). As they were filling their little hiking cups with fresh mountain water, one of them said, "Wouldn't it be great if someone bottled this and you could buy it?" to which all the other hikers laughed and said, "yeah, right – who would *buy* water?" We probably had those same thoughts as we hiked up in the Cascades when I was a kid... little did we know that silly notion would turn into a world-wide multi-billion dollar industry.

VCRs:

These are quickly going the way of cassette tapes and the old vinyl records. CDs, DVDs, etc. (digital media) are all anyone – even some of our grandparents – have now. But when I was a kid, there were very few options if you wanted to see a movie (or TV show for that matter). To begin with, you only saw a TV show if you watched it when it was broadcast on TV, and the TV I grew up with was something that kids today would never understand. Where I lived, we had stations 4, 5, and 7 (the networks), 9 (PBS), and 11 and 13 (both local). TV was only received via the rickety antennae up on our roofs; there was no such thing as cable or satellite television. And TV shows really only happened between 7:00 and 11:00 pm, then the news, then Johnny Carson, then the stations signed off. The annual Jerry Lewis

Telethon was an event! We used to stay up and watch it because it was on all night – and that was special! If a kid today tuned in to the TV of yesterday, it would hold his attention for about 5 minutes. If the lack of choices didn't completely turn him off, watching the shows we did would surely do it. We all loved our sitcom shows like *The Brady Bunch*, *Bewitched*, *Gilligan's Island*, *Welcome Back Kotter*, *Happy Days*, etc. but as great as they were then (and I maintain that they still are) they were definitely a little corny. And the dramas we watched... remember shows like *McMillan & Wife*, *Starsky & Hutch*, *Charlie's Angels*, *The FBI* (in color!), and many more? While great for their day, they were definitely a little predictable and certainly lacked in the acting department.

Don't get me wrong, I could still sit down and enjoy episodes of any of those great old shows, and I'm sure that many others my age could do the same. And the great thing is that we could watch almost any of them with our kids today and not have to be concerned about our children seeing and/or hearing some of the incredibly inappropriate things that are on TV now. I will be the first to agree that the quality and content of today's programming is better in many ways, but I also feel that there are shows that only exist for the shock factor. It makes me yearn for the days when questionable content wasn't really a problem. I don't want my kids learning the ideas, opinions, and acceptance of many of the issues and lifestyles that most of today's shows try to display as being "normal." We all got along fine without risqué jokes and inappropriate situations. We laughed at genuinely funny situations, probably got a lesson or two in how to get along with a sibling, or, perhaps we learned the benefit of being honest, even if we didn't necessarily want to be.

OK – enough preaching – I just like the simplicity and fun of the shows that I grew up with. And, as is evidenced by the endless reruns of so many of these shows, it appears that a lot of people agree with me. You know what's funny? If I sit down to watch a *Gilligan's Island* rerun, I *know* that I've seen it a bunch of times before, but I still watch the whole thing, and I still laugh at all the same things! I love it!

The bottom line is that we had to watch whatever was on TV when it was broadcast – there were no other options. As much fun as it was to watch the latest *Happy Days*, *Mork & Mindy*, or *Monty Python* (the sketch comedy show was all the rage on PBS in the '70s), it was even more fun to recite all the funny one-liners with your friends at school the next day. If you missed it, there wasn't the option to watch it on a VCR or DVD later. And – if you were lucky enough to see a movie at the theater (not a massive Cineplex with 8, 12, or 20 screens, but a single screen that showed one movie at a time), it was a real treat. If you missed it in the theater, it would probably be a couple of years before it would be on TV and of course it would be chopped up by commercials. No; we didn't have VCRs and DVDs when I grew up, but we enjoyed TV and movies together and at the same time as the rest of our friends and family.

CDs (Digital Audio Media)

We still call them records; we still talk about an artist's latest record; but when was the last time that any of us actually played an LP on a turntable (hip-hop scratching not included). More importantly – how many of us have replaced all of our favorite LPs with CDs? And – many of us proba-bly have all of our music stored on our computer hard drive and backed up just in case.

There is something that the CDs of today don't offer, or at least they don't on the scale that the old LPs did. A great way to spend an afternoon was listening to your latest and/or your favorite album(s) with your friends, and a big part of that experience was looking at the album art and reading the inner jacket. There was so much cool stuff to read! The artists would often write some great personal comments and insights. There were pictures of concerts and recording sessions – remember – you couldn't just jump on the web and google (Did you know that "google" is apparently a verb now?) images to see pictures of your favorite artist from the day he was born up through this morning's news conference. Other than what you saw in a few teeny-bopper magazines, this 12" x 12" collection of images and writings was your only window into the secret lives of your singing idols.

Technology is wonderful and the advancements made in audio with the introduction of digital recording has taken music to a whole new level. We had to tiptoe around the living room when listening to our LPs for fear of bouncing the record player. It was such a bummer when your favorite album got its first scratch, which was inevitably followed by more scratches, and because it was your favorite album it usually got worn out first. You became accustomed to listening to it knowing that a familiar click, pop, or hiss was now forever part of your copy of the song. These days, you can listen to your CDs as you barrel down the highway or even negotiate a bumpy road and never hear anything except perfect music. And – if you do happen to "skip" it, it doesn't even cause any harm to the CD. They aren't totally inde-structible, but since you probably have it backed up on your computer, if something does happen to it, you can just burn a new copy that will be as perfect as the original.

Today we toss around our CDs; throw them in the glove box on our driving trips; pop them into our players while we're working out, at work, etc. And I haven't even mentioned iPods, MP3s, etc. that can digitally store thousands of songs. Most certainly, the days of carefully stacking your LPs on end so they wouldn't get hurt, enduring the scratches, and reading the liner notes while listening to it in your home are all but gone. I know that we all appreciate the technological advances available to us, but I will always cherish the mem-ories of the simpler days of the big vinyl albums, the 45s (and those little plastic yellow things that you had to use with them), and all the excitement that owning them brought us.

Computers:

I know… I'm *seriously* overstating the obvious… but we did not have personal computers when I was a kid. Computers were the thing of futuristic science fiction movies. And really – they only ever seemed to be used by "evil geniuses" for their "take-over-the-world" plans. The idea that I, or any of my friends, would ever have anything even *closely* resem-bling a computer only crossed our minds when we were also dreaming of a Utopian future with flying cars and robots that did all of our chores, ala "The Jetsons."

I remember in 7th grade I had the opportunity to take a typing class. By that time electric typewriters had been introduced, IBM Selectrics to be exact. Remember the little "typeballs" that twisted at incredibly high speeds and punched the tri-colored ribbons? It was pretty cool to watch, but I could only make it move that fast if I typed like this: "qort1owhfo-qwnf;oqweo;wqey"… and it wasn't cool enough to make me take typing class – that's for sure! You see, by this time I already knew I wanted to be an architect when I "grew up." I was planning on making a living by drawing! I laughed under my breath at all the losers who were thinking of almost any other type of career who *had* to take typing. I did not ever need to be one of *them*, or so I thought.

For many years this was the case – almost all the way through my college years. Soon, typewriters got more sophisticated, and then they became something called "word processors." They had a little TV monitor called a "screen" and they could actually store your information on them – on these little magnetic floppy diskettes. This got me a little more interested in them, but I still didn't need them to be an architect. But, in 1982, a little company called AutoDesk started offering a program that could use computers to draw lines and do some very basic drafting functions. And, they used a machine called a plotter to produce these drawings in a form that resembled what I drew on my drafting board. Well – I don't need to drag out this entire history – except maybe to say that I should have bought AutoDesk stock, and we all should have bought Microsoft stock – but that's a whole other story.

I – like most everybody else these days – use my computer in virtually all aspects of my life. And, like my cell phone, I can't imagine how I could function in life without it. Oh sure, when I go backpacking and I'm up enjoying the Cascades for a week, I seem to do just fine without it. But in my every day life, it's my brain backup these days. A quick scan of my files shows me that I have folders for each of my family members. We have documents for shopping, back to school info, a variety of packing lists, letters, reminders, financial documents, etc. We have thousands of digital photos as well as thousands of songs from hundreds of CDs. We use it to pay many of our bills and talk to all of our friends and family members. I have hundreds of AutoCAD drawings representing dozens of homes I've designed. We have résumés, organization info, copies of important documents, calendars to remind us of important events and to help us track scheduled services for our cars, appliances, etc. We use the Internet extensively for everything from product research to shopping to entertainment to the latest news. My computer is an essential part of my life. And, yes – I do have a separate hard drive backup. If you can relate to this description, make sure you have a backup, too. (Hey, hey… free computer consultant advice ☺.)

I don't think that kids today can even begin to fathom what life would be like without computers and the Internet. It is amazing to find out that there are websites for just about everything that you can imagine. And we truly do live in the information age. You can find out almost anything with just a few clicks in a search engine. I fear that kids today won't know how to use a dictionary, won't know how to use an encyclopedia, and won't know their times tables since the handy little calculator is so easily accessible. While it's true most of these kids can run circles around us using the computer and can figure out how to use new programs faster than most all of us, I kind of wonder what would happen if they had to survive without one. Maybe the whole world would slow down and we'd all take time to look things up, talk with each other, and physically write things down.

By the way, I never did take typing lessons. I'm not fast, but I can hold my own and definitely do much better than "hunt and peck."

Shoes with Air in Them:

I'll have to admit that I have never owned or worn a pair of Air Jordans or any other high-tech tennis shoes. And I've certainly never spent more than $40 for a pair of tennis shoes. I'm not sure they're even called "tennis shoes" any-more. Perhaps they are now called some sort of "foot enhancement device," or "physical performance augmentation accessories."

The point here is that we didn't buy nor were we given ordinary things that cost extraordinary amounts of money.

In today's world, it's not uncommon to have what looks like very normal clothing – or for that matter, what looks like old and/or worn out clothing – that costs more than my mom would've shelled out to dress all four of us kids for "back to school!" Had my mom known that all she had to do to get us ready to make a big impression on the first day of school (oh yeah, like she really cared about that… but if she did…) was to outfit us in the worn-out, faded, weathered (read "distressed" in today's vernacular) clothes of ours that she *was* going to give to Goodwill, she would've been one happy woman! She could've bought a whole new set of curtains with all the money she saved – actually, to more accurately reflect what she probably would've done – she could've bought the material to *make* a whole new set of curtains.

Fashionable purchases were something for the stars and the "jet-set" society, not for kids who were begrudgingly plodding back to an institution of education with their minds still running around the neighborhood engaging in every type of fun they could still cling to. Well – OK – maybe we did want to have a pair of "waffle-stompers" or "star-jeans" or a cool down vest, but if we actually got something like this, it was from JC Penney, and usually towards the end of the fashion trend when they were on sale. The only exception to this being that we all HAD to have swabbies (a type of jeans), and in Seattle, we HAD to buy them downtown at the Army-Navy Surplus Store. You weren't cool if you didn't have these. We didn't have the shopping options kids have today. There weren't any weird shops with loud weird music with weird clothing lines with weird names where we could shop! There wasn't a social expectation that compelled us to beg our moms to invest a small fortune so we could have a certain "look" when we went back to school. Overall, we didn't think too much about fashion, especially as boys. Now it seems that the entire essence of who and what a kid is is, in part, determined by the clothes he wears, where he got them, and how much he paid for them.

I don't know where else I could insert this – but I really have to ask – what is it with kids and their pants today? I mean – we had our crazy fashions – striped pants, wide legs, bell bottoms, elephant ears, plaid pants with huge cuffs, platform shoes, silk shirts with huge lapels and entire mountain scenes printed on them, corduroy suits, etc. But at least our clothes covered us up! If you're a kid today, how do you even shop for the pants you wear? "OK… let's see… my butt's totally hanging out – albeit covered with underwear; I need to keep pulling them up so they don't fall down; I can't even walk normally because they're so restricting… they're PERfect!" I know that I'm embarrassed every time I see a photo of the clothes I wore when I grew up. But I think that the kids today will *really* have to wonder what they were thinking when they look back on photos of themselves years from now. I mean – how do you explain that one to your kids?

I think that the money that is spent on kids' fashions today is ridiculous and borders on being criminal. It's only possible because society has set the bar so high and made it un-cool to do anything other than tightly hold onto that bar as you traverse the social levels of your young life. Clothes weren't really a fashion issue for us growing up... never really was a part of our thought process... just something that we wore. Our moms don't know how good they had it.

Now, obviously, this is a guy's perspective. My sisters have both made it very clear to me that fashion was very important in their world. There were a lot of items that were "must-haves" in their social circles.

My oldest sister said that saddle shoes were a *must* in grade school. Also pleated plaid skirts, white blouses (with as little lace as possible), and cardigans that match the skirts were very popular. Ponytails were all the rage and charm bracelets were very cool, and the more charms the better! Apparently it was best if they had a special story, too. She got hers at the 1962 Seattle World's Fair. Our Grandmother would solder on the new charms when she got them. She still has it today and it has a lot of charms that she got from the Fair.

My other sister said that she remembers that culottes (today I think they call them "skorts") were really popular. She remembered girls being sent home in 7th grade because they wore them. They looked like skirts and had to be closely inspected to determine that they actually were culottes. The teacher's suspicion would only be aroused when the girls were whispering amongst themselves. Now isn't that ridiculously ironic? The more modest clothing item was taboo and a girl wearing it would be punished.

Water Parks:

It was a real treat to go to the public pool when I grew up… a big step above the local lake. There were two diving boards – the low dive and the high dive. One of the greatest poolside status symbols a kid could have was being able to dive off the high dive. Whether or not you performed a perfect dive wasn't important. Unless you accidentally laid out for a perfect belly-flop, which would only cause your peers to laugh at your pain, you always gained respect for diving off the high dive. However, one of life's biggest mysteries as a kid was how high the high dive actually was. From the ground, it would look like anyone could dive off the high dive, but once you got out at the end of the board and peered down at what was *easily* a 50-, or even 100-foot drop, there was no way you were going do anything riskier than just a regular jump, or *maybe* a cannonball. When I faced this situation, I would decide to leave the diving to the athletic kids and just end up doing some pathetic little jump – while holding my nose, of course – and then dogpaddle my way back to the shallow end to maybe join a splash fight.

It was fun to try to imagine that we were causing some sort of real problems with the pool if we could actually get our finger or thumb to block one of the inflow jets of water. And it was always fun to try to swim to the bottom of the 12-foot deep end before our heads would cave in from the pressure.

If you wanted to play in the water while running around, you ran though the sprinkler in the front yard at home. The regular oscillating sprinkler was the standard fare. A bit of a twist to that was the ones that swirled in a circle... it was even more fun to jump through. And the best, of course, was if someone had a water wiggle. These were a lot of fun. The toy consisted of a seven-foot plastic hose attached to an aluminum water-jet nozzle that was covered by a bell-shaped plastic head. When the water was turned on, the little plastic head – complete with a happy face painted on it – would rise up in the air and wiggle all around due to the water pressure. They were an absolute blast as they chased us around the yard.

Today, the kids have water parks! They're actually a great idea. Take the fun of playing in the water, and add to it the fun of playing in a park, and make a *water* park! These are huge expanses of pool playgrounds. They have half a dozen twisting and turning slides, rivers to float down in oversized inner tubes, playful showers, jets of airborne water to run through, and many other very creative ways to play in the water. Families now can make a day of it: hours of playing in the water for the kids; nice lawn chairs for mom and dad to nap in the sun; concession stands that offer treats and even hamburgers and hot dogs for meals. What used to require planning ahead and packing (equipment and food) now just takes three little things: a decision of which water park to go to, a bathing suit, and a checkbook (or debit card!).

Water parks are great fun, but they take away from the adventure that playing in a lake provided, they squelch the creativity that playing in your front yard required, and they make any local pool boring by comparison.

Lawsuits Around Every Corner:

One of the saddest things about life these days is the fact that there is such a huge dark cloud of concern over having to be careful with everything you say and do. As I've said, I'm all about safety when and where it's necessary, but I've heard of some of the most ridiculous lawsuits these days in the name of "safety." There's a grade school in Oregon that banned the game of tag at recess because it "encourages fighting." They've also convinced Portland public schools to get rid of swings, merry-go-rounds, tube slides, and teeter-totters because they're too dangerous! There are "T-Ball" games now where every kid always gets a hit and they don't even keep score! The overriding fear is that of litigation! What's really sad is that it's not so much a concern that the kids might get hurt, as it is a fear of lawsuits. We all had more than our share of scrapes and bruises growing up and with each one we all learned a lesson or two and – if we were lucky – a big dose of common sense. No, today – it's all about litigation. Americans have seen too many sensational-ized stories in which people who have been "traumatized" by something – whether it's a hot cup of coffee that burned someone, or a kid crying and pouting because his delicate lit-tle psyche was hurt when he didn't win a prize even though he came in last place. As a country, we are achieving medi-ocrity and complacency due to our refusal to defend the notion of common sense!

I love Corvettes. Did you know that a warning is sewn on their sun visors about not putting your baby in a car seat in the front seat because of air bag deployment danger? Really? A *Corvette*? How many moms are transporting their infants in their Corvettes? It's just amazing that the fear of litigation has made it so everything and anything has warnings all over it. Where will it all end? Pretty soon, there will be a *Life for*

Dummies book out that will have to cover everything that you could ever do wrong. At least it seems like that's where we're headed.

So, the next time you let your kids' friends climb the tree in your backyard, or think about doing a good deed by helping someone who gets in a fender-bender, or try being a good citizen in some sort of incident, remember – you are putting your entire estate in potential jeopardy. Gone are the days when at least a "thank you" or maybe even a token of appreciation would be extended to you. Instead, you might be summoned to a court hearing where you get to explain why you were not at fault for... well... whatever it is that you did or didn't do.

Cell Phones:

These started to be available publicly in the mid '80s, but they were so large that they couldn't be carried around easily. In the early '90s they started getting smaller, and of course you know how small and powerful they are now. How great, in today's world, to be able to have your kids check in with you all the time... whenever! Growing up, we had one phone per

house... *maybe* two. They were all rotary dial – you know – little dials with holes by the sets of letters that you had to spin and then let it click back. It took a long time to dial anyone. It always seemed that if you had a number to call that had a lot of 8s or 9s, you'd try to hurry it up and always mess up on the last number... and then you'd have to do it all again. The 1-button speed dial was something that we couldn't have even imagined. Can you imagine trying to use a rotary phone to call in on "American Idol" to vote for your favorite contestant? They'd have to extend the voting period just because it would take everyone so long to dial!

We also had something called party lines. Private lines cost more. This was another area where my folks could save some money. I don't remember it being an issue more than just a few times, but it was a reality. You'd pick up the phone to use it and somebody else was talking on it. It was a little weird if you think about it now, but there were some other families – *some*where – that used the same phone line as you. I guess it worked because we all used the phone so much less in those days. We did crazy little things like *walking* over to our friend's houses to see if they could come out to play, or *going* to the library to see if a book we wanted to check out was back in yet. We didn't just call anyone and everyone about anything and everything; we actually got out and physically engaged ourselves with people and spent time with them. We only had party lines when I was really young, but I remember them well.

Another thing was making long distance calls. In addition to being very rare and expensive, these had to be done by using the operator. There wasn't even an option to "direct dial" long distance calls. You had to dial "0" and then the operator would take the number and place your call. And if you were calling collect (which meant the person receiving the call had to pay for it) you had to sit by while the operator asked if they would accept the charges. It all seems so funny now, but it was the only option we had then.

Many kids of today might not know that we had prefixes that related to our switching office or phone exchange. This meant that our phone number was LIx-xxxx, instead of 54x-xxxx. The "LI" stood for Lincoln – our switching office. I don't know why this was, or exactly when it ended, but I do remember reciting my phone number as a kid by starting with "Lincoln...." It was a good thing that we did have those switching office prefixes or we would never have had the great 1940s piece "Pennsylvania 6-5000" by The Glenn Miller Orchestra. And, of course, in the '80s, Tommy Tutone made use of phone numbers without the alpha prefix with their hit "867-5309."

Here's something funny we did. When my dad went on business trips, or any of us went away on vacations without everybody else, we wanted to call home to let everyone know we were OK. But we didn't want to have to pay for the long distance call. Since we had to go through the telephone operator, we would call and ask for ourselves. You know – my dad would call and ask for himself, and we would refuse the call since he wasn't home. But we knew through this system that he had arrived safely. If he wanted to talk, he would ask for my mom and we would accept the charges. It seems silly now, but it was an effective way to avoid long distance charges that added up rather quickly back then.

I have a cell phone. I can't imagine how I could effectively live life today without it. Between communicating with family (immediate and extended), using it at my job, communicating with my clients for my side job, and calling in to vote for "American Idol" (I admit it – I have done this), it has become an essential part of my life. I'm sure most of you reading this feel the same way about your cell phone. It's funny how something that was invented so recently is now so critical to all our needs. We may not have had cell phones when I was a kid, and we survived fine without them... but... I'm glad we have them now!

Cameras:

In 1978 I bought a "real" camera – a Pentax K-1000! An SLR! This was a huge step up from anything that anyone in my family had ever owned (you know, the Kodak instamatic with the little blue square flashbulb cube thingy on top that twisted when it flashed?) and I really enjoyed it! I still own that camera and have only recently fully stopped using it. The pictures that I could take with it were incredible. I could manipulate the light, add filters for effect, attach a zoom lens and get some great shots, even use magnifying lenses to shoot things up close! I have photo albums full of years of great shots. The one thing that was always a  treat was getting the pictures back from the developers; just the anticipation of waiting to get them back was an integral part of the process. And then we would sit around with friends or family and look at how all the shots came out – that was half the fun of taking pictures. The good, the bad, the surprises, the disappointments… you never really knew what you were getting until you opened up the package.

Compare this to the situation today. Digital cameras are cheap (as in inexpensive), well-made and easy to use. They come in all shapes and sizes; you can get them on your phones, in your pen, in a wristwatch, and even in a lighter. You can take hundreds of pictures, see them instantly, and then choose which ones you want to keep. You can edit, crop, colorize, add special effects, take out red eye, enlarge, reduce, reverse, etc. You can store all of your pictures on your com-puter. It won't be long until most of us won't even know what a negative is anymore. I take pride in the fact that I've managed to keep all my years of photos and negatives well organized, but that whole concept will soon be a thing of the past. All of our photos will be stored digitally and probably only a small amount of them will even be printed. Most of our pictures are emailed and viewed on computers.

Gone are the days of everyone gathering together and passing around the pictures from the last family gathering, putting your initials on the back so you can get reprints made for you. It's a whole new digital world. It's much more convenient, much better quality and much easier. It's a little piece of life that will never be the same.

As I've shared – there's a lot we didn't have when I grew up. We didn't miss what we didn't have, and of course, what didn't exist yet. We certainly lived life at a bit of a slower pace, and I think we enjoyed the things we did have a little more because we spent more time at them. All the things that we have available for us today are great. Don't get me wrong, I'm not wishing the world today was just like it was back then (mostly) – just pointing out how different it was.

Chapter 4

Things We Had and Took For Granted

Growing up in the '60s and '70s was a completely different experience from anything kids of today could even imagine. I will be one of the first to admit that all of us – as we look back at experiences of our childhood – are probably prone to remember things better than they might have been. But, I will also be one of the first to assert that – for the most part – life really was good back then. This got me thinking about how there were a lot of things that we didn't think twice about as being completely normal and that we may have taken for granted.

Our Parents:

For almost everyone that I grew up with, we all had our original parents! For those of you who grew up then, how many kids did you know who came from a broken family? I think that I can remember one kid in my grade school – and his father had died or was in jail. I'm sure there were more as I progressed through junior high and high school, but it's hard to even come up with a handful of names. I don't need to try to find some statistic to quote about how many, or rather, how few kids today live with both of their original parents. We've all heard those depressing numbers. But, back then, it was a rarity. I think the fact that so many of us grew up in the atmosphere of an intact nuclear family helped us develop into a pretty well-balanced generation with adequate social skills and a sense of responsibility to ourselves and others. Mom and Dad were always there. Life wasn't always perfect, but they didn't just call it quits when problems arose.

Mom Was Always There:

When we got home from school, mom was there. We had after-school snacks, we played, we did our homework, and mom was there. We didn't have to let ourselves in; we didn't have to stay at a friend's house; we didn't have to hide inside and avoid answering the phone. She greeted us at the door or at the bus, helped us out of our wet clothes when we got inside, wrapped a warm blanket around us, plopped us down in front of the fire with a plate full of freshly baked Nestlé's Toll House cookies and turned on the after-school special for us. Well, maybe that's stretching the truth just a *little* bit. The point is that we had the safety and comfort of our mom when we got home each day.

Home Cooking/Baking:

The reason that our moms were there when we got home from school is because they didn't work! I mean… at a job outside of the home! Lord knows they worked harder than all the rest of the family members put together, and there ain't NO one who would dare to argue that point. Without a doubt, our moms made some of the *greatest* meals. They may not have been the fanciest meals, and by today's standards, they probably had a little too much good ol' fat in them, but they were great and we loved them. My mom was a casserole queen, as were probably most of our moms. What better way to feed a bunch of kids affordably? And it was easy enough to make extra to have enough leftovers for dad's lunch or another meal. Great food and good times sitting around the table at dinner.

Many of our moms also did canning. At least a couple times each summer my mom would invite my aunt over and they'd spend all night making blackberry jam. There isn't anything that can duplicate the smell of fresh blackberries right off the vine being cooked up and poured into those sterilized canning jars… and then the smell of paraffin being heated and poured to seal them up. There is nothing better than homemade blackberry jam, and we got to have it year 'round. What a treat – we never realized how good we had it!

My mom was also an incredible baker. She made pies, cakes, and some of the most awesome Christmas and holiday treats. Her real specialties were blackberry pies, shortbread and fudge so smooth that it melted in your mouth. I'm sure that most of you have moms that are also great cooks/bakers. Today – for no other reason than just because you love her – call your mom and thank her for all the years of great food.

Walking to and from School:

We didn't have many concerns about walking to and from school. There was a whole bunch of fun to be had on every trip. Whether it was trying to find a new route so you could beat everyone else, or finding some treasure as you poked your way home, there was hardly a concern for safety. However, I do remember that we had two areas that we always were a little leery of whenever we passed them. And our childhood imaginations made these places bigger than life and almost scarier than our little psyches could handle.

The first place was where "the old man" lived. My sister said that we called him "monkey-man." We didn't know anything about him and that made him all the scarier. His house was so overgrown with trees and bushes such that we could barely see it, and we **did** hear monkeys. I swear – we did! It doesn't make sense now to say it, but I know we heard monkeys back then… in the house… right by the road – um – in the middle of suburbia. Whatever. It *was* a scary place, even though we hardly ever saw the guy.

The other place there was the "witch's house." As is obvious to me now, this was nothing more than an older house that was set back off the road, and happened to be in some tall trees that creaked in the wind. But it was this setting that convinced us that the woman, who we may or may not have ever actually seen, was definitely a witch. In spite of what seemed in our eyes to be irrefutable evidence, I don't know that there was ever *anything* to give us any real reason to believe that the woman who lived there was a witch. She never appeared in a long black dress with a tall pointy hat. There were no unexplainable flying broom sightings, no glimpses of her hunched over a boiling cauldron muttering "bubble, bubble, toil and trouble." But in our minds she was a witch nonetheless.

But you know what? Those were the only places where we were afraid. We had no fear walking through all the other neighborhoods on our way to and from school. It may sound simple, but it was a given fact that it was generally safe to walk outside, even alone. Sometimes the trip home was filled with some discovery or some fun diversion. There's the potential of a whole different world of things to look at and experience in an everyday walk to and from school, but because it's not safe, kids today miss out on this as they are driven both ways every day. I don't blame the parents; it's just a sad commentary on the condition of our country today.

Dinners at Home:

 I read recently where kids eat dinners at home an average of three times a week. I would wager that the majority of those dinners are while sitting in front of the TV and are probably not with all of the family members at home. And how many times is that dinner a real home-cooked meal? When I was growing up, it was rare that we did not have dinner at home; rare that we weren't all there; and rare that we didn't have a home-cooked meal. We went out to dinner only on special occasions, and we dressed up to do it, even if we were just going to Denny's or Big Boy's. Eating out was a special occasion and we treated it as such! This may sound really funny – but it was a real treat to have TV dinners at home. This is when there were only one or two brands, they were a novelty (and pretty terrible, I might add), and it really was fun on the rare occasions when we got out the old metal TV trays and actually sat in the living room to watch TV while we ate dinner. We felt like we were living the high life.

With today's work-a-holic parents, fast-paced lifestyle, epidemic levels of single parents, fast food, and everyone having more meetings, committees, teams, classes and events, etc., dinner at home – especially with the whole family – is more of a rarity. Dinner at the table was a time for the whole family to sit down together and talk – not necessarily about big important stuff – just a time to catch up on the day. But it was one more thing that defined and built us together as a family. We also learned some valuable life lessons. We learned that it was fine that we didn't like what was set in front of us, but we still had to eat it. Not many of us kids chose the option of going directly to bed after dinner instead of just eating something that we didn't want. Mom was very good about our meals being healthy, balanced, and nutritious. Not that she worked especially hard at it, she just knew how to cook good meals and did so all the time.

Safety:

My daughter was born in 1989. When she was young, I wouldn't think of letting her go outside at night to play with her friends, even if it was in my own backyard. I would be concerned about anything, everything, anyone, and everyone that might walk or drive by. For that matter, I would feel it necessary to keep a very watchful eye on her if she were outside with her friends in the daytime. And never mind all the unknown factors from *outside* my neighborhood – there were people right in my own neighborhood that I didn't know – what about them? I'm almost ashamed to have to say that this is my mindset, but it's one that is dictated by these times.

Conversely, I can remember what seemed like endless summer nights of playing hide-n-seek, kick-the-can and other games until 10 or 11 at night with a handful of my neighborhood friends. And the area we lived in didn't even have streetlights until I was a teenager. Sometimes, we would quit the games and just lie on someone's lawns watching for a satellite (a REALLY rare thing in the '70s) and maybe tell ghost stories. When our parents would finally call us in – we would all head home for the night, but we knew that we could look forward to repeating this same type of fun many more times that summer.

We (or more importantly, our parents) had little fear of kidnappings, drive-by shootings, drug dealers, or the many other sick things that threaten the streets of even our nicest suburbs today. Making sure that we were safe was the reason that our parents lived in the suburbs to begin with. The neighborhoods were a safe place. We didn't have Block Watch programs; they weren't necessary; a neighborhood was a natural block watch program. We all probably had what we considered a couple of surrogate moms where we could always go and visit whether our friends were there or not. And, best of all, the kitchens of these other homes were as open to us as our own.

It was in the Seattle area that product tampering first happened (you remember – the Tylenol scare) so ever since that time we've had safety packaging. In the '70s, it didn't even cross our minds to wonder if the food we bought from the grocery store was safe to eat, especially the pre-packaged stuff. Safety packaging has developed its own place in our culture as the butt of so many jokes about the difficulties it imposes on us all, especially the elderly. What was intended to protect us has ended up mainly causing us frustration in our simple every day activities. How many times have you had to open anything from a pill bottle (line up those hard to see arrows) to a jar of peanut butter (can you ever get all of that foil off of the jar rim?) and ended up having less than pleasant thoughts towards these otherwise harmless, inanimate objects? I'm sure that I'm not the only person who has muttered a few words out loud at these things thinking that somehow they will succumb to my verbal assaults. Oh well, this is the world we live in, and I believe that the protection that we have these days is great. Too bad it's necessary.

Resources:

The first major oil crisis hit in 1973. That was the first time that I was really affected by a shortage (created or real) and saw and experienced its impact. I remember how weird it was to actually have to be in line for gas. Although I wasn't driving at the time, I remember that it was a big deal and that a lot of people were pretty upset about it. My dad and mom were incredulous about the whole thing. It affected me more in the pocketbook when I bought my first car, because by that time (about 1977) the cost of gas had risen from 30 to 60 cents a gallon. Boy – wouldn't we love to have those prices right now? But back then it was unbelievable that we had to pay that much money for a gallon of gas.

Neighbors/Neighborhoods:

I've already talked about how neighborhoods were inherently safe, but there was also a feeling of family, and a security in knowing the people who lived next door. I'm talking about parents chatting over fences, kids having milk and cookies or homemade popsicles next door, moms borrowing cups of this and that from each other, kids being watched by the neighbors at the drop of a hat. All these things were commonplace in my neighborhood. There was an unspoken care and support between all of us and it wasn't something that we "signed up" for. Don't get me wrong... the Block Watch program that is in neighborhoods is great, but sadly, it's a necessity. Today, many of us tend to be alienating ourselves from each other. I could probably hypothesize on dozens of different sociological and psychological reasons that may or may not have caused this, but the bottom line is that people today seem to be less trusting and more suspicious of others. I feel fortunate that I grew up being family friends with our neighbors and being able to trust them or go to them for help.

People Being Considerate of Others:

My folks were fortunate enough to buy a house in an area just north of Seattle that had a spectacular view of Puget Sound. My dad told me about the day that someone finally bought the lot across the street and my folks got really nervous. They were concerned that they were going to lose their view when the new neighbor's house went up. The new neighbor turned out to be a contractor, and as my folks were able to meet him, he let them know that he was aware of the view they had and would make sure to construct his home so it wouldn't block their view. And that's just what he did; even coming over to stand on our deck during construction to verify that his roof ridge was below our line of sight. That's just the way people were back then – considerate.

Fast forward to 2001. That's when somebody else bought the house and decided to do an addition. The "addition" was another whole floor added to the top of the already two-story home! As opposed to the original builders, these people seemed to hide from my folks, and apparently never even considered what they were doing to the view that my folks had enjoyed for over 40 years. While they didn't have any legal obligation to do or say anything to my folks, common courtesy would cause most people to at least have a conversation about it.

Common Courtesy:

Manners. Respect. These seem to be concepts that are foreign to many of today's kids. Of course, I need to stress that I'm not lumping all kids together in this assessment, but there seems to be a much higher percentage of those with a lack of these qualities. Kids today say and do things to adults that I would never have dreamed of doing. We addressed adults as "Mr." or "Mrs." or "ma'am" or "sir"; we were polite to strangers; we paid attention when spoken to; we didn't mumble through conversations. There were unspoken rules and expectations. We didn't talk when the teacher was teaching in class. We did get up and give a woman a seat on the bus. We didn't call someone's home phone number after 9:00 pm. We did say "please" and "thank you." I'm sure that we weren't perfect – probably far from it – but the attitude we had was much different than what I see today.

And another thing – didn't you all write thank-you letters to your grandparents or out of town family for the gifts they gave you at Christmas or on your birthday... at least up until you were a teenager? I know we did. We had to! And while we didn't really have a choice in the matter, we did learn to be grateful and express our appreciation appropriately. Now, I am not at all against email. I mean, let's face it... it's not just a fad... I think it's here to stay. BUT (OK – time for me to get up on my soapbox): just because we can email does NOT mean that we should all lose our ability to spell, write complete sentences, and use correct grammar. AND – we do not get to change entire sentences and expressions into single letters and combinations of punctuation marks in every email we write! I am continually amazed by the emails that are sent to me on a professional level that would cause most English teachers to faint, or at least throw in the towel on their profession. I will concede that "texting" is an acceptable medium in which to use this sort of "writing," but it shouldn't be used anywhere else. (OK – I'm getting down off of my soapbox now.) Do yourself a favor – if you have young kids, make them put actual pen to paper when they write letters. It will be good for them.

A Little Piece of the American Dream:

We didn't have anything special growing up in the way of a big house, fancy cars, vacation homes, etc., but we did have our little piece of the American Dream. While this really didn't amount to more than a modest home, the property it was on, and a not-brand-new vehicle or two, it was all we needed for our family to live a successful life. As kids we learned to do without when it came to not getting everything we wanted, and we all took our turns in the hand-me-down chain – even among cousins and neighbors if the opportunity arose.

Today, it seems like kids get everything they want and then some. I have seen kids – and I mean young kids – decked out in all the latest fashions and toting the latest in personal electronics. Families seem to have big nice new houses, new sporty cars and SUVs, and don't really appear to be lacking anything for their lives. It seems like the little piece of American Dream concept today is more of a "we deserve to have the best of everything" attitude. The idea of going without seems like it's not even an option. I know that there are more families in debt now than ever before, and I think that it's probably becoming epidemic. I don't believe that owning our little piece of the American Dream should come at a cost of high consumer debt. When I grew up, we worked for and earned everything we had. We lived a very simple yet real level of the American Dream, but we didn't go beyond our means to achieve it.

Good Guys/Bad Guys:

I am not naive enough (although, don't ask my brother on this one) to believe that things were perfect when I grew up. I guess, though, that I had a belief that in general, things were handled fairly in the world of good guys/bad guys. One thing that stands out for me was that – for the most part – the good guys looked and acted like good guys, and the bad guys looked and acted like bad guys. With the exception of spies, you could pretty much count on being able to tell a lot about a person by his appearance.

This seemed to hold true in most everything – politics, sports, entertainment, and everyday life. I don't think that it was until the early '70s, until shows like "Shaft" came out, that I remember thinking that it was "cool" to look "bad." I know that I'm probably way off base, and there were probably dozens of other examples prior to that, but I just remember that was when *my* perceptions started to change. Shaft was a really mean, bad, against-the-norms-of-society *cop* – a *good* guy. I didn't even see the movie until many, many years later, but was affected by it when it came out. And – it seemed the world had been, too. There were more and more examples of what appeared to be good guys being bad, and those who looked scary-bad being good. Of course, today that line is totally blurred... nothing is guaranteed to be as it seems when it comes to first impressions. We have so many examples in every possible aspect of life where things and people are not as they seem. So – it was pretty easy back then – the good guys wore the white hats, and the bad guys wore the black hats; the good guys wore suits and ties and were clean shaven – the bad guys were unkempt and unshaven; the good guys smiled and were helpful – the bad guys leered and were mean. Whether or not it was all true, it seemed easier to tell the good guys from the bad guys.

Growing Up with Neighbors/Friends:

People move a lot more now than I remember when I was a kid. I was born two weeks after my folks moved into the house that my Dad still lives in. I graduated from high school with many of the same kids who were in my kindergarten class. Many of the parents of my high school friends still live in the same houses they did when we grew up. Some of the people I grew up with did move away, but most did not. I think that the reason for this is that when we grew up, most of our dads worked with one company for their whole career. It didn't matter whether they worked for IBM, a position in city government, a local store, or a big national chain... most of them kept their same jobs. As a result, a lot of us crawled, toddled, learned our ABCs, ate 12 years of school lunches, endured boring assemblies, and ended up graduating together. Our friendships lasted for years, even extending beyond high school. I recently went to my 30th high school reunion, and we had close to 300 people there. For a graduation class of about 700, that's a pretty high turnout. It was great to see everyone and reminisce about those old days growing up together.

I still chat with and/or see some of the same neighbors that I grew up with when I go to visit my Dad. I think that having the solid background of my neighborhood and friends, along with a stable nuclear family, has given me a level of stability in life that many of today's kids will never have the benefit of experiencing.

Chapter 5

The Music

I was talking to my sister the other day. She had just been on the phone with her 20-year-old son who had just gone to a Bob Dylan concert and we ended up talking about how interesting it was that the kids of today know so much of "our" music. There's just no denying that the music of the '70s was some of the greatest music ever!

It would be impossible for me to try to list all of the incredible songs, the incredible bands, or the incredible soloists from the '70s. Just a bit of late night channel surfing will probably land you on more than one '70s music offer. There're the "Love Songs," the  "Classic Rockers," the "Soul Collection" – and many more. There was a lot of just plain good music produced in those years.

While I don't think that I need to give examples as proof of this, all you have to do is pay attention to the music in today's movies to see how popular they still are. It blows me away how many times the majority of the background music in movies is from the '70s. And what about TV commercials? It's obvious that these days Madison Avenue is pandering to my age group. The commercials for the new (retro) Mustangs and the new Cadillacs – just to name a couple – are chock full of great '70s music. When was the last time you attended a major sporting event (assuming you are fortunate enough to do so) and "YMCA," "We Will Rock You," "Hells Bells," or some other '70s song adopted as a modern day sports anthem *didn't* play? It's always amusing to me to see old ladies dancing and doing the YMCA moves to a song by the Village People… I don't think they know too much about that group.

We can't talk about the music of the '70s without bringing up everyone's favorite, disco! Hold it – don't throw the book down in disgust – I know that there was a lot of disco that really kind of sucked. And – suffice it to say that almost all of the fashions that came out of the disco era were crimes in and of themselves. I think that late night TV commercials that sell disco music should issue a statement prior to the start of each show warning of extreme laughter due to some of the clothes they wore. And if the fashions themselves weren't funny enough, the colors were so extreme that the images were permanently burned on your retinas for hours afterwards. Of course, because it was *the* popular music, many of the big singers back then threw their hats into the ring and released their own disco songs, which probably did more to damage than further the cause of disco. Despite this, and the outrageous fashions, there were a lot of amazing disco songs and some incredible artists. Donna Summer, Le Chic, The Spinners, The Bee Gees, etc. Songs like "Boogie Oogie Oogie," "Love Hangover," "Car Wash," "Dancing Queen,"

"Knock on Wood," "Last Dance," "Bad Girls," etc. I dare you to not sing or at least hum along if you are driving and "Celebrate" by Kool and the Gang comes on the radio.

Do you remember *The Midnight Special*? If you stayed up past Johnny Carson on Friday nights, you were in for a real treat. It was 90 minutes of taped in-concert popular music. I was up flipping through the channels recently and saw a special on late night TV where they've put together a package of DVDs of the show! Wolfman Jack (one of the great radio DJ's of the day) was the announcer and there were different guest hosts each week. The show highlighted the week's latest and greatest Rock & Roll hits and showed their performances, along with usually having one of the bands on the show. We didn't realize how incredible it was that we could see all of these performers doing their hit songs on a weekly basis. This was long before the concept of MTV, and these weren't video productions – they were performances – like a small concert with a bunch of different artists. It was what "American Bandstand" was to the '50s. Someday I might decide to shell out the money, call up a bunch of my friends, and sit down to watch and reminisce about the good music that was a part of our lives.

There were a lot of big solo performers back in the '70s: Elton John, Rod Stewart, and Billy Joel to name a few. What's amazing to me is how many of these guys are still performing today. We're talking 30 – 40 years of hits and a prominent place in music history. And bands – there are many bands that were huge even through the '80s, but took a decade or so off, and now they're all coming back. You can catch a lot of them in the local casinos, or at summer concerts where usually 2 or 3 perform together. It's awesome to see some of these guys performing again... and they've still got it... they do a pretty good job of dancing around and being pretty energetic for their 50-60-age range. And, of course, there are some big name bands that haven't ever slowed down. The incredible Rolling Stones being the epitome of rockers who just won't quit, and haven't made the mistake of going beyond that point where they should've quit.

Here is a (**non** all-inclusive) list of some of the successful bands and soloists of the '70s just to get your feet tapping and your memories flowing (disclaimer – I know that everyone won't agree that these were all great, and some people will probably gag on some of the names listed. The wide variety of music means some of you won't even relate. We've all got our own opinions of what was good, lame, etc. However, I think that we can all agree that the decade did produce some incredible music):

ABBA, Aerosmith, Al Stewart, The Alan Parsons Project, Alice Cooper, Ambrosia, AC/DC, America, Aretha Franklin, The Association, The Average White Band, Bad Company, Bachman Turner Overdrive, Badfinger, Bad Company, Barry Manilow, The Bee Gees, Billy Joel, Black Sabbath, Blondie, Blue Oyster Cult, Bob Seger, Boston, Boz Scaggs, Bread, Captain and Tennille, Carly Simon, Carpenters, Carole King, The Cars, Cat Stevens, Chicago, Dionne Warwick, Dire Straits, Deep Purple, Donna Summer, The Doobie Brothers, Earth Wind and Fire, Eagles, Eddie Money, Electric Light Orchestra, Elton John, Emerson Lake and Palmer, England Dan and John Ford Coley, Englebert Humperdinck, The Fifth Dimension, Foghat, Foreigner, Gordon Lightfoot, Grand Funk Railroad, Grateful Dead, Guess Who, Hall and Oates, Heart, Helen Reddy, Jackson 5, Jackson Brown, J. Giles

Band, James Taylor, Janis Ian, Jefferson Airplane/Starship, Jim Croce, Jimmy Buffet, Joe Walsh, Journey, KC and the Sunshine Band, Kansas, Kenny Loggins, Kenny Rogers, KISS, Kool and the Gang, Little River Band, Leo Sayer, Linda Rondstadt, Loggins and Messina, Looking Glass, Lynard Skynard, Mac Davis, Marshall Tucker Band, Meatloaf, Molly Hatchet, Neil Diamond, The O'Jays, Olivia Newton John, The Osmonds, The Partridge Family, Pat Benatar, Peter Frampton, Pink Floyd, Pointer Sisters, The Police, Queen, The Raspberries, REO Speedwagon, Rick Springfield, Rod Stewart, Rolling Stones, Rush, Santana, Seals and Crofts, Sister Sledge, The Spinners, Steely Dan, Styx, Sweet, Supertramp, 10CC, Talking Heads, Ted Nugent, The Temptations, Toto, Van Halen, Van Morrison, The Village People, The Who, U2, Yes.

And these are some groups or individuals that had some really great hits in the '70s but got their start in the '60s:

The Allman Brothers, David Bowie, Cheap Trick, Eric Clapton, Fleetwood Mac, Jethro Tull, The Kinks, Led Zeppelin, Lou Rawls, Moody Blues, Ray Stevens, Simon and Garfunkel, Steve Miller Band, Steppenwolf, Stevie Wonder, The Supremes, Three Dog Night, ZZ Top.

Please don't start yelling at me as you read through this list. I know that I missed some, and I might have missed your favorite, and I probably included some that you can't stand. This will probably be the one place in this book that I keep running back to with last minute edits.

Incredible music, incredible bands, and an incredible experience – that was the '70s! Just google "'70s Bands" and you can spend a few hours reminiscing and remembering the good times. Caution: you may be very tempted to start replacing all your old vinyls with CDs or some other form of digital media! And – take it from me – it can get expensive!

Chapter 6

The Movies

Recently, my wife and I thought we would share with our daughter what had been one of the most impactful movies of our lives as we grew up, *Brian's Song.* I remember so clearly how my whole family had bawled when we watched it, and my wife had similar memories of when she watched it. As Brian Piccolo lay on his deathbed in the hospital, his friends and family were in the room grieving and one by one gave their last respects. Well – the impact of these moments was almost totally lost in the almost laughable quality of the acting and production of the movie. Now – I need to be very clear here – there is nothing wrong with the movie and in its day it was very powerful. I loved the movie, and as I said

before, both my wife and I had cried when we had watched it as kids and it was etched in our minds as one of *the* movies from our time. But to compare the quality of movies from then to that of today is like comparing Chevettes to Corvettes. While they're both cars, they aren't even in the same league.

I was not at all surprised that my daughter was not as affected by it as we had anticipated. There is no way to compare today's movies to the movies we grew up with. There were certainly great classics that came from years past, undeniably great movies and performances that will stand the test of time. But compared to the sheer volume of movies today, and the quality of special effects and production capabilities it makes it hard for the older movies to compete for the attention of a younger generation.

A friend shared with me the other day that she remembered when watching a movie awhile back she suddenly realized that she wasn't amazed by the special effects in it. And it wasn't that they weren't amazing, it's just that she had reached the point where she was taking it all for granted. It was all done so well that she didn't have to try to imagine it any more. In talking with her about it, we realized that our kids have often taken much of what they see for granted. They've never had to suspend belief while watching an obvious model or miniature scene and make a conscious decision to believe it.

When I was a kid, it seemed like there were a few movies put out every year... and I do mean a few... that's all. Now it seems like there are a few movies put out nearly every *week-end!* Certainly, when volumes are increased to that level, there are a lot of low quality, very forgettable, and generally stupid films. Even so, the mass marketing techniques available today can help to make even these a slight financial success. So – there probably won't ever be a decrease in volume. And there's always the chance that a low budget sleeper will be a totally unexpected success (*Princess Bride* and *Napoleon Dynamite* for example).

I remember when *Star Wars* came out in '77 – the original one – how it was *the most incredible film ever!* And it was!

There had never been anything like it. As I was a bit of a Sci-Fi buff, I saw it 11 times within the year that it played at the UA Cinema 150 in downtown Seattle. Again – if you wanted to see it – you had to go to the theater to see it. In contrast, I now pick and choose which movies I see in the theaters, since they are out on disk within a month. Some people even have home theaters that rival the big screen. Not me – yet (some day, I hope to ☺) – but you can get almost the same experience without having to ever go to a theater.

I still love to go to the movies; I love to watch the big-budget, fast-paced, action-packed films. It's a luxury that is afforded to the kids of today that was not even thought of as being possible when I was a kid. I'm grateful for the movies that I could watch when I grew up, but they are nothing when compared to what the kids of today accept as being normal – and possible.

I must add that there were some incredible movies from the '70s - there were some real classics. Following is a list of some of the ones I remember, or like, or just know that they were big movies. I don't necessarily endorse these, I have seen a fair amount of them, and there are some that I will never see. Nevertheless, this is evidence that there were some really good movies back then, not just ones that I *thought* were really good:

Alien, American Graffiti, Animal House, Assault on Precinct 13, Apocalypse Now, Blazing Saddles, Butch Cassidy and the Sundance Kid, Cabaret, Carrie, China Syndrome, Close Encounters of the Third Kind, Death Wish, The Deer Hunter, Deliverance, Dirty Harry, Dog Day Afternoon, Escape From Alcatraz, Fiddler on the Roof, The French Connection, Funny Lady, Grease, Godfather, Goodbye Girl, The Great Gatsby, Hair, Halloween, Harper Valley PTA, Jaws, Kramer vs.

Kramer, Logan's Run, Love Story, Mad Max, M*A*S*H, Monty Python and the Holy Grail, Murder on the Orient Express, Network, Norma Rae, One Flew Over the Cuckoo's Nest, Paper Moon, Patton, Pink Panther (4 movies), Planet of the Apes, The Poseidon Adventure, Rocky (2 movies), Rocky Horror Picture Show, Saturday Night Fever, Smokey and the Bandit, Star Trek, Star Wars, The Sting, Summer of '43, Superfly, Superman, 10, Taxi Driver, That's Entertainment, Tommy, Towering Inferno, Where the Red Fern Grows, Willy Wonka and the Chocolate Factory, The Wiz, Young Franken-stein.

A lot of these would be a good rental, although – again – I'm not necessarily endorsing them. In many ways, these are nowhere near the caliber of the production of movies today because the technology just wasn't there. But many of these movies reflect the changing social and highly charged politi-cal climate of the late '60s and early '70s and are – as a result – powerful movies in their own right. And I know that there were plenty of "dirty" movies in the '70s, but you had to watch them purposely in order to see some of the stuff that seems to be readily available in even PG movies today. Back then, movie stars kissed with their mouths shut. At least, they did in the movies I watched. Touching someone else's tongue with yours was called French kissing and they didn't do that in movies. I don't know what they did in French movies, because we didn't watch them. There seems to be a lot of promiscuity, innuendos, and sexually suggestive con-tent in even PG and PG-13 movies today. There are a lot of good movies from when I was kid, and they will always remain classics in their own right.

Chapter 7

The Toys

Gameboys?

Our games were creative. We folded a regular piece of notebook paper in a somewhat complex pattern that ended up in a triangle. With this, we spent the good part of an hour playing "football" on a table in the library on break. You know... hang it over the edge of the table for a touchdown; put your forefingers together, thumbs up for a goalpost – like two guns facing each other; stand the football on one corner and flick it between the other guy's "goalpost."

Electric Light Sabers?

We had sticks... and we made the sounds with our lips.

Toy Guns?

We did everything we could to make our toy guns look real. The coolest ones were made out of scraps of wood. We would use a handsaw to carve in a crisscross pattern on the handle; glue little "sights" on the end of the "barrel" (usually a piece of an old broomstick); and then wrap the whole thing in black electrical tape – maybe even paint it all black. Our goal was to make it look as much like the real thing as possible.

Today this could get you in a lot of trouble. I recently heard about a kid at a middle school who was shot by the police when he pulled out his toy BB gun. Apparently, in an attempt to make his gun look as real as possible – he had painted the telltale orange tip that identifies it as a BB gun, black. So the police didn't recognize it as anything but a real gun. It's sad that now BB guns need to be "marked" so that they will be recognized as not real; it's an even sadder fact that the threat of kids bringing real guns to school is so prevalent. Gone are the days of my youth when all the boys would gather to show off the knives they got for Christmas at recess in the school-yard, or bring the BB gun for Show-and-Tell.

One of the most realistic toy guns that we did have was cap guns. They were really fun and were pretty loud. Although expensive, one of the greatest things to do with caps was to take a big rock and drop it on a whole roll of caps. Nothing like the smell of gunpowder to make you feel like you shot a real gun!

The Sears Catalogue Christmas Wish Book:

As winter approached and the daylight got shorter, my brother and I would play inside more and more. And, as Christmas got closer, we started to dream of all the neat toys that there were for us to dream about. We had at our finger-tips one of the greatest tools available to us at the time: the Sears Catalogue Christmas Wish Book. We would grab the big book soon after it came in the mail and plop ourselves down on the living room floor... faces in hands and eyes all agog at the treasures inside. We had to get by all the boring pages of clothes, appliances, and household items, but then we got to the endless pages of kids having what seemed to be almost unfathomable fun as they flew, built, created, raced, colored, threw, and in every conceivable way, *played* with all of the incredible bright shiny toys that were offered in the full color pages. It was obvious - these kids were experiencing a level of fun far beyond the limits of our understanding. They all had perma-smiles plastered on their faces and were dressed and groomed like all good kids were. There wasn't a hint or even the slightest suggestion that they were doing anything but being the types of kids that all parents dreamed about. In fact, half of the time their parents were looking on in seeming admiration of their children as they employed these wonderful toys as a means of endless entertainment. While our eyes and minds were filled with these wonders, we didn't often get much of what was there. As I mentioned before, there were the occasional larger single presents – which were often shared with our siblings – but the Sears Catalogue Christmas Wish Book is where we went to dream about what might have been.

Commercials:

Saturday morning was the day that kids watched cartoons. Back in the '70s, the average household was filled with kids laughing at the funny situations that were depicted by the animated cartoons of the day. Today, it seems more likely that after a Saturday morning of watching cartoons, kids minds will be filled with them envisioning themselves as renegade loners (or possibly part of a misfit group) that defies the norm and most likely doesn't recognize an authority figure or set of laws that pertain to them as they seek to right what they see as wrong, and often in the name of some "greater good" that remains suspiciously vague in definition.

Oh, brother! What happened to the *Bugs Bunny/Road Runner Hour*? What about Underdog, Super Chicken, George of the Jungle, the Jetsons, Foghorn Leghorn, Marvin the Martian, Mushmouse and Punkin' Puss, Tom and Jerry, Atom Ant, Speedy Gonzales, SlowPoke Rodriguez, Heckle and Jeckle, Limpy the Lion and Hardy Har Har, Popeye, etc.? You want to make yourself laugh right now? Just try singing your favorite song in an Elmer Fudd voice! I was blown away a couple of years ago when I heard that in today's "enlightened" society, almost all of these would be deemed as "unsuitable for children to view because of their violent nature and the confrontational message they conveyed." I would be much more concerned about a small child wanting to model themselves after a "hero" who dressed provocatively – or at best, in a skin-tight leotard, possibly employed other shady characters and operated on the edges of the law to "fight for something greater than us all," than I would of some cat and mouse bonking each other with mallets a few times. I think that there's a much greater chance that kids would get the "hero" and reality mixed up than they would grab mallets and start hitting each other.

OK – so I got a little, no, a *long* way off track. The point that I was going to make in all this is that watching the commercials on Saturday mornings was one of the best ways for us to be introduced to all of the cool new toys and the latest sweetest cereals that were available. The manufacturers knew their audience and knew where we would be on Saturday mornings. I know this is still the case today… Saturday mornings are definitely prime time for kids watching TV, and they've all got their eyes glued to the boob tube the whole morning – just like we did. Good ol' American commercialism will ensure that TV commercials are used for educating kids on the latest and greatest toys for a long time to come.

Thinking about this made me remember all of the advertising icons that we grew up with. I'll just list the character, you can try to come up with the product (some are obvious): Sugar Bear; Tony the Tiger; Snap Crackle and Pop; Cap'n Crunch & Jean LaFoote; The Maytag Repairman; Mr. Whipple; Mrs. Olson; Madge; Mr. Peanut; The Marlboro Man; The Doublemint Twins; Trix Rabbit; The Jolly Green Giant; Sprout; The Pillsbury Dough Boy; Morris the Cat; Count Chocula; Colonel Sanders; Betty Crocker; The Keebler Elves; Quisp and Quake; Frankenberry; The California Raisins; Boo Berry; Dig'em the Frog; Toucan Sam; The Leprechaun; The Kool-Aid Pitcher; Ronald McDonald (and Mayor McCheese, The Hamburglar, etc,); Nestlé's Quick Bunny; Hamburger Helper Helping Hand; Pillsbury Funny Faces – mugs – Choo Choo Cherry, Holly Olly Orange, Goofy Grape, Rootin' Tootin' Raspberry, Loud Mouth Punch, With it Watermelon, Lefty Lemonade, Rutti-Tutti Frutti and Freckle Face Strawberry; Coca Cola Polar Bears; Hamms Beer Bear.

And what about the slogans and jingles? Knock it off. I dare you!; Let Noxzema cream your face, so the razor don't; Maxwell House - Good to the last drop; Folgers – Mountain grown for better flavor; The best part of waking up is Folgers in your cup; Candy coated popcorn, peanuts and a prize; You deserve a break today; Meow, meow, meow, meow; When you say Budweiser, you've said it all; I'd like to teach the world to sing; Baseball, hot dogs, apple pie and Chevrolet; Ancient Chinese secret, huh?; It's not nice to fool with Mother Nature; I can bring home the bacon, fry it up in a pan; Libby Libby Libby on the Label Label Label; Ho, Ho, Ho; Hey Mikey! He likes it!; Come to the Honeycomb

Hideout; Put a Tic Tac in your mouth and get a bang out of life; Wouldn't you like to be a Pepper, too?; Sometimes you feel like a nut; A is for Apples, J is for Jacks; My baloney has a first name; Plop plop, fizz fizz, oh what a relief it is; N E S T L E S, Nestlé's makes the very best, chocolate; Hold the pickle, hold the lettuce; Sorry Charlie; Ask any tuna you happen to see; How about a nice Hawaiian Punch?; Who wears short shorts?; Taste fit for a King; Mona?!?; I can't believe I ate the whole thing; Hey! You got chocolate in my peanut butter; No more tears!

Recently, one of the TV stations started running what they call "'70s Retro-mercials" on TV. They actually run some of the old commercials from back then. It's so cool to see them again and they bring back some great memories.

We all owe a debt of gratitude to many of the classic cartoons that gave us all massive exposure to the incredible world of classical music. You may be surprised to know that you can probably hum the main parts of Richard Wagner's "Ride of the Valkyries," "Carmina Burana (O Fortuna)" by Carl Orff, and "Peer Gynt Suite No. 1 'Morning'" by Edvard Grieg. In addition to the identifiable pieces, there are countless others and all the fill-in music that were the background throughout each cartoons. While we didn't know it, we were all given a classical music education. We might have been too busy laughing at our favorite characters' escapades to realize it, but the music was being recorded in our minds.

Hot Wheels:

There was *nothing* cooler than Hot Wheels and we all wanted them. There were two reasons that we were able to really get

into them when we were kids. First off, my Dad's job had paid well enough that my brother and I were the proud recipients of one of the "double super-charger" sets for Christmas. These had what seemed like miles of track, plenty of curves and **two** of the super charger units. Believe me, we were the envy of the neighborhood for a while once we got them! Secondly, we had a grandmother who drove her car quite a bit, and Shell gas stations had a promotion where every time you purchased at least 8 gallons of gas, you got a free Hot Wheels car. We loved visiting her and receiving a handful of cars every time. Mattel did such a great job of making some really outrageous designs. Our minds were filled with the possibilities of these fanciful cars as we packed them into their display cases and dreamed about owning *real* hot rods!

We spent many a Saturday or Sunday afternoon setting up huge tracks and running our cars through the paces. When there was a pile-up on the track, we just kept on sending bigger and faster cars to break up the piles. We played *hard* with our Hot Wheels, and they showed it. It pains my heart now (in the pocketbook chamber) to surf on over to eBay and see some of the cars that we had once owned in pristine condition selling for large amounts of money. I saw single rare cars going for between $1,000 and $1,500; and there were whole collections selling in the $3,000 - $4,000 range. If ours were still in new condition, we'd have the possibility of amassing a small fortune from eager collectors. I've toyed with the possibility of selling what we do have – there would still be a fair amount to gain, even in their well-used condition – but I've really enjoyed the times in recent years of pulling the set out and looking it over. Brings back a flood of good memories.

Our close friends up the street also had a huge set of Hot Wheels. We would have a sleepover and fill their entire recroom with both of our sets and spend endless hours playing with them. I know that you can still buy Hot Wheels today, but they aren't near the draw they once were – too much high-tech and electronic competition. For us, they were one of the coolest toys that we ever had. They provided hours and hours of fun, and probably led a lot of us to eventually own muscle cars… I know they led me that way.

Lego's:

Another fun toy we had growing up were Lego's. These were the same idea as the long time favorite Lincoln Logs – giving kids the tools and opportunity to build and create. Lego's were great because you could buy small add-on sets and additional pieces to add to what you already had. In my day, though, there weren't nearly the options there are today. We basically had blocks in the standard sizes, shapes and colors, some flat pieces, some wheels and a few pre-defined shapes. Today, you are able to buy kits that have the pieces and shapes you need to put together different types of planes, cars, machines, etc. While I think that they are still a great thing in that they provide the chance for kids to build something with their hands, these sets with pre-designed objects do take away some of the creativity that Lego's used to offer.

The problem with owning Lego's as a kid is that no matter how hard you tried, it never seemed like you could pick them all up when the order came down from Mom to clean your room. If I had a nickel for every time that a member of my family, did the "I just stepped on one of those stupid little Lego pieces in my bare feet" dance, I'd be rich. They also seemed to be able to migrate about the house on their own. Even to this day, when I visit my folks' house, it's not uncommon to come across a Lego block in the bottom of some old drawer.

I have some friends that went to Lego-Land a few years ago. There were *huge* displays of national monuments, room-size scaled city street scenes and tons of other cool things all made with Lego's. These sound like they would have been incredible to see. I wonder what guy – who was probably a kid the same time that I was – got the awesome job of building Lego's displays for a living? Talk about a kid's dream come true!

Pong:

There's something that we all need to realize: every single one of the incredible video games that are available to us today all started with Pong. It doesn't matter if your game of choice is the latest war game or the most spectacular sci-fi game; or whether your free time is spent playing solitaire on your computer or computerized elementary educational games with your kids; it all started with Pong.

Pong was a pretty simple concept. The home unit was a console with a couple of dials on it. Each of the two players used a dial to move a little vertical dash on their side of the TV screen up and down to bounce a "ball" between them. It was like tennis on TV. It was the first home video game that we could buy and play at home. We were very fortunate that my dad and mom actually bought this for us. We spent hours on end lying on the floor playing Pong. My dad even set up tournaments for all of us to play each other. We were mesmerized by the game because we'd never seen anything like it. By today's standards it would have trouble holding the attention of any kid for more than a few minutes. In retrospect it didn't have too much going for it. It was monochrome, had just a couple of "beep" and "boop" sounds, and was pretty slow paced. But – back then it was high-tech, cool, and a lot of fun!

Models:

When I grew up, a lot of kids I knew built models. World War II airplanes, Navy ships, lots of cars. It was a whole experience. We took a long time to decide which model to actually buy. And we had to get the real models, not just the snap together ones. Cars were a lot of fun to build, and we always did some really cool paint jobs on them. But ships and planes were the coolest! The ultimate was to build a sailing ship with all the rigging, a real challenge, but very rewarding.

Once we had picked out which model to build, we had to prepare to do the project. The kitchen table was the best place to work but we had to have a lot of newspaper down. Nothing like the wrath of mom to put the fear in you about spilling model glue on the table. Models were one of the best things that I did to teach me patience. Lots of little parts and pieces; detailed instructions; exact assembly sequencing; I couldn't rush the process; and I had to commit a fair amount of time to do the entire project. My favorite models to build were cars, being a car enthusiast, and I used to take a lot of time to really do a good job on them.

My friend and I would try to customize the car body in some way, and then we would get flake paints and do custom 2 and 3 layer paint jobs. I still have some of those models at my parents' house. On the flip side, there was a horrible fate awaiting the models that didn't turn out well, got broken beyond repair, or were just not ones that we wanted to keep. Firecrackers! We were able to... um... acquire these at a nearby Indian Reservation. We had a lot of fun destroying these unfortunate models. Some very creative things can be done with firecrackers and models. I'll never forget when my brother and I and some friends sent an old model of the Enterprise Aircraft Carrier to its demise with an M80. We found pieces of that thing half a block away! Yes – models gave us all sorts of entertainment – for both our creative *con*-structive and creative *des*tructive outlets.

General Toys:

Without taking the time to go into detail on all of the other cool toys that I remember, I'll just mention of a few of them:

Army Men – What kid didn't have dozens of these and probably blew up more than a few?

Barrel of Monkeys – "A barrel of fun."

Electric Football – This game was all chance – a vibrating metal plate and plastic men.

Etch-a-Sketch – Hey look, I can do stairs!

Magic Window – by Wham-o.

Nerf Football – Mom always said, "don't play ball in the house…"

Operation – Ha, ha, ha!

Rock 'Em, Sock –'Em Robots – Knock your block off!

Rubik's Cube – I still don't know anyone who could actually do this.

Slinky – "It's fun for a girl and a boy"

Spirograph – OK, it came out in the late '60s, but it was so awesome!

Stratego – My brother *always* beat me in this.

SSP's – Pull the ripcord, and they were fast!

Toss Across – Remember? You threw little beanbags and flipped the x's and o's – it was a giant game of tic-tac-toe.

Vertibird – the most incredibly fun, battery-operated helicopter ever!

Treat yourself to a trip down memory lane and google '70s toys – you might even get inspired to go see what you can find in your parents' attic!

Chapter 8

The Cars

Ok, hold your hand up in front of you, make a fist and look at the thumb side of it. Stretch out your forefinger and thumb and now – put them as close together as you can without actually letting them touch. You know – like saying "this much." That's how close I came to **not** being integrally involved in one of the greatest decades for cars.

In 1971, my dad bought a brand new Datsun 510 sedan for $1,800. The thing ran forever and he drove it over 350,000 miles needing very little more than regular maintenance. When I graduated from high school in 1977, it was time for me to start looking for my own car. It made sense for me to start looking at something like my dad's car. By now, Datsun was producing the "stylish" B-210, and it would be the perfect car for me to purchase. It was brand new, had the latest in Japanese car comforts, got great gas mileage and came with a great warranty. This should've have been a no-brainer.

But... I had a friend.

He was a close friend who could identify the year, make and model of any car just by looking at it. He could describe to you the differences of the successive years of any model of any make. But more importantly, he loved big American cars, especially big gas-guzzling sporty American cars. He already owned one (a '71 El Camino) and he was very concerned that I would consider buying anything less than a similar muscle car. I was facing a major possibly life-changing decision: do I follow in my dad's footsteps, make the smart-money decision and buy a car based on value and economical performance, or do I take the advice of my friend and start down the road of owning a car for its looks and high performance?

Common sense vs. Classic Chevy, and the winner is… let's just say that I had the hottest '73 Camaro! (Yes, that's a picture of it on the cover.) I almost bought a '73 El Camino with a huge 454 cubic inch 4-barrel, an incredible paint job, and Crager SS 5-spoke chrome wheels. Once I started looking at something other than a "sensible" car, I got really excited about Camaros. I ended up buying a '73 in the Fall of '77 for $2,950. Oh – and can everyone relate with me that I bought my own first car? The only help I got from my parents was that they co-signed on the loan… none of this "buying-your-kids-a-car" nonsense.

Within a year of purchasing my car, I had already decided that I wanted to paint it and make a lot of changes and improvements. My friend and I decided that we wanted to show our cars. To make a long story short, I spent a lot of time – and especially a lot of money – on it. We did show our cars at the Seattle Center Coliseum for 3 or 4 shows. It was a real trip, a whole lot of fun and something that I'm really glad I did. In retrospect, there is nothing that compares to the feeling of being slammed back into your seat as you stand on the gas of a big ol' Chevy V8! Add to that the fun of cruising in something that turns everyone's head, rumbles even when it's just idling, and looks fast just sitting still, and I don't regret for one minute the choice I made back then.

I do love the incredible cars of the '70s. What's amazing now is to see what some of these cars sell for. It's not uncommon to see Chevelle SSs, Camaro Z-28s, Road Runners, Challengers, Barracudas, El Caminos, Chargers, Novas, Cougars, Corvettes, Mustangs and Mach 1's, for 30, 40 even up to100K if they're all stock and in perfect restored condition. There are also a few that sell for more including Pontiac Superbirds in the 200K range. Man – if we only knew then what we know now!!! I think when I finally got rid of my Camaro back in '89, I got $700 for it. The only way I would have come out ahead is if I'd taken that money and invested it in Microsoft stock back then. But I already talked about that, didn't I?

It's great the way that all the car styles from the '70s are starting to turn up again in the latest cars. Mustangs, Chargers, Thunderbirds, even the new still-to-come Camaros and Challengers are being based on the '70s models. There was something about having a muscle car that *looked* like a muscle car that made all the difference. If you want to start drooling over some of these classic beauties, head on over to eBay and do some looking. Or, visit the Barrett-Jackson auction website. You'll probably start kicking yourself as much as I did when you see what your old car would sell for now.

Chapter 9

Family Vacations

Our family took a lot of summer vacations. By that I mean that we went camping almost every weekend. Since we lived in western Washington, it was just a short jaunt up to the Cascades where we would camp, hike and fish. It wasn't that much further to eastern Washington where we would stay in campgrounds on the mighty Columbia River and spend our days playing in the water. And we also went camping in and around the San Juan Islands. I was fortunate to grow up in a beautiful area that offered a lot of opportunities for a family to enjoy nature in its fullest beauty.

I think that camping is one of the great American traditions. My family has only been "tent" campers. Not only is this – in my opinion – the *only* way to camp, but when one is a  tent camper, one is automatically at odds with all of the "campers" in trailers, campers, Winnebagos, etc. My brother, cousins and I wandered and laughed and pointed at these people who were really only trying to get out and enjoy the great outdoors in their own way. In our judgmental and sarcastically youthful eyes, they all tended to be overweight and lazy. We adopted the "weebles" jingle as our musical description of them in general. You know – "Weeble's wobble but they don't fall down, all they do is roll around...". We felt that being tent campers automatically put us in the superior position in the realm of all campers because we were roughing it and closer to nature, sleeping on the ground, subjecting ourselves to the wilds of the outdoors more than everyone else. Truth be told – we didn't have the money for the resources that all those others had, whether or not we would have bought them, but we did learn an appreciation and understanding of nature, and more than a few life lessons in our camping adventures.

What may seem like an obvious life lesson that you could learn from camping is "don't feed the bears." Right? What may *not* seem so obvious a lesson, that I learned, was "don't chase the bears with pots and pans." One of our camping trips was in Yellowstone National Park. This was back in the days when you could just drive there and camp without having to sign up on a waiting list a year ahead of time. We had arrived in the evening, set up camp and had turned in for the night. My brother, cousin and I were lined up in our sleeping bags outside, dad and my sisters were in the tent, and my mom had claimed the comfort of the station wagon with the seats down to make a nice bed. Sometime in the middle of the night there was a bunch of noise at the picnic table in our camp. Frantic flashlight sweeps of the camp revealed a bear helping itself to whatever food it could find in our stuff. This created the expected screams and scrambling for cover in all of us... except my mom. Apparently, we'd been there a few years prior to this and suffered the same lack of hospitality from another member of the Yellowstone bear club. We'd lost our ice chest in that encounter and my mom wasn't about to let that happen again. So while we all, including my dad, jumped in the car or the tents for safety, mom surveyed the situation and decided to take stock of her arsenal. The most vivid memory I have is that of my mom clanging her pots and pans together and moving *towards* the bear. By the response of the bear, it seemed that this was not an uncommon reaction to his campground visits. He glanced her way but didn't really stop his search for a treat. He had just succeeded in opening the ice chest and had found the object that had lured him there… cocoa butter! We used it back then as a soothing lotion on sunburns, and it smelled just like chocolate. Whether it was because he had found what he had come for, or because of my mom's incessant pot clanging and yelling, he decided that he'd had enough. He took his prize and lumbered off. Surveying the damage afterwards revealed that while the ice chest survived, what food was left inside was beyond salvaging. Mom's pots had a few dents but nothing that couldn't be pounded out. My brother, cousin and I were really scared when we saw footprints showing the bear had walked right across the bottom of our sleeping bags on his way to the table. We had slept right through it, which was probably a good thing. The incident still causes my father to shake his head and wonder about the sanity of the woman he married, and the kids retell it to brag about our mom taking on a bear. And while she was successful in her endeavor, we learned that chasing down bears in a campground wasn't a good thing to do and that we should never, ever attempt any similar feat.

Another life lesson we learned while camping was to take the time to understand the far-reaching effects of a single action. We were camping at a city park/campground in a little town in eastern Washington and had a nice big corner lot with beautiful cottonwood trees all around us. My brother and I, being typical boys, were playing with matches. Looking for stuff to burn, we noticed that the ground was all covered with a layer of snowy white fluff. We didn't have cottonwoods where we grew up so this was all very new to us. We scooped a bunch of it into a pile, bent down and lit it. The way it whooshed up in flame surprised us. We grabbed another handful and lit it to make sure it wasn't just a fluke and were delighted to see the same results. This was really cool! We ran toward mom and dad excitedly telling them we had something that we had to show them. As they met us, we saw that the ground at our feet was thick with the stuff. We uttered the words "watch this..." and (I don't really know if it was my brother or me) dropped a lit match onto the ground. In retrospect, in our defense, I know that we were as innocent as we were stupid. If either of us had taken even a second to think it through, or if we'd given our folks just a few seconds to respond, we could have avoided the whole thing. If you know the cotton from cottonwoods, you know what happened next. Instantly there was an ever-expanding ring of fire racing out in all directions at our feet. As we all realized what was happening, we started trying to stomp the fire out. It was a dry day. We spent the good part of the next 15 minutes racing to every corner of our camp trying to stomp out the fire. The highlights of the event were realizing that it was almost underneath our car, seeing that it was almost to our tent, and hearing Grandma screaming that it was almost under her lawn chair. When we had finally stomped out the last of the flames, we were standing in a blue haze with everything intact but our dignity. I don't remember if there were other campers or not – I don't recall anyone helping us – but I'm sure that our antics gave anyone within sight of us a good laugh. Probably gave them all a good story to tell to their family and friends, too. The full lesson we learned was to take a minute to think things through before you do them, and pay attention to the consequences of even the smallest act.

We also usually had one "big" vacation each summer. These were usually 2-week long driving trips that our family typically took with my Dad's brother and his family. Destinations ranged from the Oregon Coast to Disneyland to the Grand Canyon, Arizona, Yosemite, Yellowstone, Glacier Park, The Great Salt Lake, Lake Tahoe, etc. With the two families, an occasional friend or two, and sometimes a grandmother in tow, we numbered anywhere from 6 to 15 on these excursions.

Traveling on our vacations was always, well, how could I put this, challenging? My family grew up with the epitome of the '70s family automobiles – station wagons! And, we also epitomized the "loaded for bear"  concept with three in the front seat, three in the middle, and me and my brother in the back in a "camp" made by my dad for us. This, of course, made it necessary for us to have the huge vinyl cargo carrier filled and strapped to the rack on top. And I remember that before we had a nice vinyl carrier, dad wrapped plastic tarps around our stuff and it would come loose and flap in the breeze. We would be asked to watch the shadow of the car as we drove so he could pull over and re-secure the tarp if necessary. It was a good thing they made American cars solid back then. We stuffed them full and drove on some roads that certainly tested their durability.

And speaking of big American cars, there are a lot of things different in them today. When I was a kid, seat belts were something that we used very seldom, if at all. About the only time we consistently used them was when we went on these big trips. For some reason, it seemed like this was what they were made for. It usually took a considerable amount of time to find them, having to dig them out from down between the seats. And there were only lap belts… no shoulder belts. The seatbelts were really hard to operate, too. We had to thread the little nylon belt through the metal clip if it had come undone (and due to its lack of use, you can bet that it was often undone). Then we had to lock it together and pull it tight. If we were lucky, it would actually hold instead of slowly slipping loose.

When we stuffed more than nine people in a nine passenger station wagon, it's obvious someone was going to be left out of the seatbelt loop – usually the little kids standing/sitting on mom's lap in the front seat or the kids lying down in the cargo space behind the middle seats. We used to take turns lying on the floorboard in the back seat, head on the hump to sleep as we drove down the highway. It was very comfortable (we were little); the droning of the car lulled us to sleep while the natural heating from the floorboard kept us warm.

Being cramped up in a car (and definitely NOT a luxury car) for hours on end with your family members could make for some pretty trying times. Today, a lot of families have mini-vans or high end SUVs with all the bells and whistles. Adjustable leather seating with lumbar support, individual seats or sculpted bench seats – all with their own perfectly functioning seatbelts, power windows and air conditioning. And if you aren't tired enough to be caressed to sleep by the smooth supportive seats and the perfectly tuned suspension, there's a veritable plethora of entertainment options today: DVD players (individual movies if you want – either your own player or you can… doesn't *this* sound funny?… watch the headrest); iPods/MP3 Players (perfect music – thousands of songs – from a little thing that's *way* smaller than a bread-box); and of course there are cell phones for calling all your friends, or spending hours texting "your bff, Jill." Between all of these different entertainment options and relaxing in the luxurious accommodations, you could make an entire trip and never even know who all's in the car!

Driving trips were a *little* different back when I was a kid. First off – there was no such thing as a luxury family vehicle… luxury was reserved for the high-end sedans and sports cars. No bells and whistles or much else for that matter. We entertained 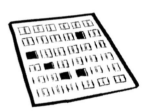 ourselves by playing road games – I think we called them car games. The Alphabet game – first one to get through the alphabet getting letters off words on signs won (first letter only!); 20 questions, which was a great thinking and logic game; we also had a fun little game called "Auto Bingo" – you might have had it, too. It was a small green cardboard card with 20 little openings with pictures of things you might see while driving. There were little red plastic windows that you would slide over each thing when you saw it. And just like Bingo, the first one to fill in a row on the card won! We also passed the time singing songs – there were a few stan-dards that we sang, and a few that we made up, too. We also did the whole "roll-down-the-window-and-moo-at-the-cows" thing whenever we drove by them. And we counted the cars in trains when we had to wait at the railroad crossings.

These all helped to get us through our trips. And sometimes, Dad might even relent and turn on our AM radio and we could catch a few mellow rock songs before he'd finally had enough.

There was also the whole issue of "space." The lack of air conditioning meant that if my arm happened to touch some-one else's arm, it was icky... even more so if it was your "stupid brother/sister." The very democratic way to solve this problem was to agree on an imaginary line – and we both had to stay on our own side of it. The general lack of comfort, sporadic boredom, and the fact that siblings are going to fight no matter what, meant that this only provided another way to agitate each other. We'd take turns trying to sneak our hand over the line, which resulted in more arguing and hand slap-ping, then we'd try to act like we "accidentally" put our hand over and then act all innocent when our sibling cried foul. It was all a big game, and just about the time that we were about to really start going at it, dad would turn around with a glare that would stop our hearts and bellow, "Do you want me to pull over?" and we knew that that meant we'd have trouble sitting the whole rest of the trip... so we'd finally shut up and get along.

We laugh about it now, but that was what traveling by car was like when my family went on trips. Whether it was playing car games, arguing, singing some silly songs or just looking out the window, we built relationships and experienced our trips together.

Another thing that we didn't have... air bags. As far as I know, it was something that had never crossed the minds of car designers back then. I think the main safety features of the cars that I grew up with were that the majority of them were built like tanks, and the pace of the overall population was slower such that there were fewer accidents. Baby seats didn't exist – mom carried the baby in her arms in the passenger seat.

The safety of cars today is phenomenal and I'm sure that there are far fewer deaths and serious injuries as a result of the safety features. I am all for, and completely applaud, the positive changes that have been implemented over the years, but most of us did survive our childhoods in spite of our lack of these safety features. So (and this goes out to all of *our* kids) give us all a break if we don't get our seatbelts fastened before the car even begins to move. What's second nature to you is something that we're trying to make a habit as we hit our mid-life years. Remember, it's hard to teach an old... er, I mean... middle-aged dog new tricks!

I think that I was privileged enough to go to Disneyland once, maybe twice, as I was growing up. These visits were in the midst of our long driving vacations and were definitely a highlight of the trip. Given the location, we actually had to stay in hotels when we went there, but staying in hotels isn't something that we often did. Emptying two cars full of kids into rooms, separating them, cleaning them up, quieting them down, and getting them into bed was something that our parents couldn't necessarily afford in time, money, or sanity. We didn't stay in the fancy Disney hotels back then, not that we would have been able to. No – we stayed in cheap – I mean – economical motels. We always stayed in a hotel that had a pool. Our parents wouldn't have survived unless all of us kids had a pool to jump in to cool ourselves off and expend some of our energy. Overall, though, these hotels weren't anything too special. Today families have the opportunity to stay at resorts that are almost as entertaining as Disneyland itself. I would venture to say that if they've been at all, they're destined to go a few times, and they will probably visit all of the other nearby theme parks as well. In my day, it was a rarity to go and it was something that was unlike anything else in the world.

When it came to the overall plan for long trips, my folks had the idea that if we just drove a lot, we would maximize our time at the places we'd visit. To accommodate this mindset, we often scheduled sleep times when we would just pull over, roll out the sleeping bags in a roadside park (I don't know if there were official "rest stops" back then, but if there was we sure didn't stay in them very often) and sleep for awhile. Sometimes this led to some interesting early morning surprises – like the time we found ourselves just a few yards from some train tracks, or when the park sprinklers woke us up in a very intrusive fashion. We didn't always find a convenient park or pull-off when my parents would have to stop for the night, so sometimes we would just pull off the side of the road and sleep. It was always challenging to try to sleep as 18-wheelers passed us and rocked the car – keeping us awake all night.

We didn't have a lot of the luxuries that seem so commonplace in today's family vacations, but I do have a bunch of great memories (and my folks' photo albums full of Kodak Instamatic Camera pictures) to help me recall that I saw a lot of this country and spent a lot of quality time with my family as we grew up vacationing and seeing the sights together.

Chapter 10

Family Life

As I've said before, I grew up in what was considered a very "normal" family. Dad, mom, and 4 kids (2 girls, 2 boys). As a family of 6, there were plenty of things for all of us to do to keep our household running smoothly.

A big part of our life was "chores." We didn't have anything formally written-up, but we all had assigned chores. There really wasn't any discussion or option – we had them and we did them. The interesting thing was that we did a lot of work and much of it wasn't easy. And if we did things wrong, we did them over. If one of us happened to be gone and unable to do his chores – guess what? The chores were waiting for us when we got back. Or we could do them early or ask someone to cover for us and we returned the favor.

Saturdays were also "projects" days. In the summers, these projects ranged from rebuilding a deck or putting in a new garden to painting the house. In the winters, there were areas of the basement to be remodeled, rooms to be painted, shelves or closets to be organized, etc. It seemed like we always had some project to do. These projects helped us to keep our house running smoothly, taught us to work together for a common goal and built us together as a family. In the midst of these endeavors, our attitudes as kids were probably a little less than stellar and we only saw that we were *not* enjoying some of our *fun* Saturday activities. We probably had more than a few opportunities to learn a lesson or two about getting along, being responsible, and helping whether we wanted to or not.

Saturdays were our chore and project days, and we almost always started them off with two essential items. Every Saturday we had waffles. Sometimes we also had sausage, or bacon or eggs with them but we *always* had waffles (and fruit – at my mom's insistence!). A Saturday without waffles really only occurred when we weren't home or mom was sick. The second thing that made a Saturday a Saturday was cartoons... and I mean the *good* cartoons!  We're talking "The Bugs Bunny/Roadrunner Hour," "The Jetsons," "The Flintstones," "George of the Jungle," "Underdog," "Super Chicken," "Yogi Bear," etc. I realize now where I get my silliness and goofiness. My dad was as adamant about watching those cartoons as my brother and I. The coyote failing once again to capture the roadrunner, plummeting to the bottom of a canyon followed by an anvil or some other contraption only to produce a puff of smoke and then walking away like an accordion... would send my dad into hysterics just as much as it did us.

There were two types of suburbia where I grew up. There were the really nice houses with really nice yards where everyone had really nice cars... you get the idea. And then there was the suburbia where we lived – not so nice. It wasn't *bad*, but it was definitely more of the "used" and "needs some work" area. Since we lived a bit more on the frugal side of life, as kids we learned a few of the more frugal ways to live. One of the things we would do is pick dandelions. My mom and dad had it in their heads that if we used any fertilizer or weed killer we might poison the world's water system. While there may be some truth to the fear that over-fertilizing could cause problems, their solution was to save money and not use anything. So we learned to pick dandelions! My mom would pay us up to a nickel per pail full. This is when we were a bit younger, maybe the 4-8-year-old range, but it was good money for us! We also had a great alternative to "poisoning the ground" when it came to pest control in the garden – we got a penny or so for each slug that we salted. Combine these two money-making ventures and we could rack up a half dollar each week. With a penchant for the penny candy down at the little corner store, we could easily make enough to give ourselves a good tummy ache.

I will readily admit that I am a blackberry pie snob. I have a perfectly good reason for this. We grew up in an area where there were a lot of blackberry bushes, in fact, our own property was an oversized lot with a huge blackberry patch. My mom was a master of blackberry dishes: Blackberry jam, jelly, cobbler (a la mode), and pie... especially pie. That was definitely her specialty. My mouth is watering just thinking about them! You have to know that a bunch of kids picking berries eventually turns into a blackberry fight. In those days, all the kids wore white t-shirts under our shirts – hence the name undershirts. We would take off our outer shirts and wear our white undershirts for blackberry fights. I have no idea of the logic (or lack of it) in doing this, but the result was a bunch of purple-stained white undershirts and a whole lot of fun... I mean... what better "fight" than one where you can eat the ammo?

There are some things that instantly take you back to your childhood... whether it's a smell, taste, or image... these things have such a powerful affect on our psyches. For me, one little whiff of Play-Doh and I am sent straight back... back to afternoons of sitting around our kitchen table and using the little cutouts to make all sorts of shapes. By the way – I could make a perfect snake – just by rolling it between my hands... I could churn out dozens of them! I thought I was talented, until I realized that almost *everyone* could do a good snake. And it was always fun to mix the different colors to make new... kind of... well... brown-ish colors. The memories are as strong as ever. I do know from experience that Play-Doh does **not** have a great taste to accompany that awesome smell.

We lived just a few blocks up the street from Puget Sound, and one of the fun things that we did that's probably *totally* illegal now (maybe it was then, too) was to put coins on the railroad tracks that paralleled the Sound. We'd put on a few coins, but would be lucky if we recovered even half of the coins after a train had barreled over them at 70 miles per hour. There was nothing like feeling the power of the huge locomotives rumbling by as we crouched a few yards off the track and tried to watch for our coins. I think that I've still got a few of those coins in the bottom of some old box from my childhood. Of course, things like these aren't worth anything except the memories that go with them, but that makes them valuable to me.

Working together, playing together, and making life work together. I had a great family and we had a great family life growing up. We may not have our Saturday project/cartoon-fests, or have blackberry fights, or sit around the table making Play-Doh creations any more, but we're still a close family and enjoy good times together.

Chapter 11

Real Life

This will probably be the chapter that you will flip to if you end up sharing some of these things with your friends, and you'll all yell out things like "Oh yeah!" or "I remember that!" or "No-kidding!"

You'll find things that we did or didn't do, things we said or didn't say and things we lived through and survived. All of this in spite of the current perceptions that many of these things are politically incorrect, health risks or just considered dangerous in today's world. There're also some things that were just plain facts of life for us, and situations and/or things that were a part of our everyday life that most kids today wouldn't understand.

I know that I have alluded to or discussed at length some of these things in the previous chapters, but here they are presented as concise little one-liners. Some of these are mine, some of this is stuff that is floating around on the web. I included most of the ones I could really relate to. They're not in any particular order. I'm sure that you could generate a list of your memories of the '70s just as long. If you do, send me a copy!

And, lastly, there might just be some fun memories in here,
too…

- If we failed a class, we stayed back a grade.
- We shot guns at "krauts" and "japs."
- The Oscar Meyer Wiener song had the lyrics:
  "…fat kids
  skinny kids
  kids who climb on rocks
  tough kids
  sissy kids
  even kids with chicken pox…"
  in today's politically correct world, it would be something like:
  "…weight-challenged children
  weight-challenged under-nourished children
  children who interact with the great Mother Earth
  by means of tactile interaction at natural geomor-
  phic outcroppings
  children who inappropriately express themselves
  through belligerent and often physically violent
  outbursts
  children who, through no fault of their own, are at
  risk of being belittled due to their lack of physical
  abilities, simplistic appearance and/or social
  inabilities
  even children affected by an avian disease most
  likely from an inhumanely bred, fed, and slaugh-
  tered fowl"
- The baby cribs that we all grew up in were decorated
  in brightly-colored lead-based paint. These crib rails
  are what we broke in our new teeth on – or used as
  teethers.

- Many of us survived being born to mothers who smoked and/or drank while they carried us. They took aspirin, ate blue cheese dressing, tuna from a can, and didn't get tested for diabetes.
- We had no childproof lids on medicine bottles or those pesky little plastic things (childproof latches) on all of our kitchen and bathroom cabinets.
- When we rode our bikes, we didn't have helmets or elbow or kneepads.
- As children, we would ride in cars with no seat belts or air bags.
- Riding in the back of a pick-up on a warm day was always a special treat.
- We drank water from the garden hose and not from a bottle.
- We shared one soft drink with four friends, from one bottle and no one actually died from this.
- My mom used to defrost hamburger on the counter, and I used to eat a bite of it raw, too.
- We used to take our lunches to school in really cool lunch boxes (that are probably worth a bunch of money on eBay today), or in brown paper bags. We never had icepack coolers, and none of us ever got *E. coli.*
- We all took gym. We wore white t-shirts, white gym shorts and white tennis shoes and all did the same activities. Things like calisthenics, running lines, and climbing that stupid rope! And flunking gym was not an option.
- None of us were ever told that we were from a "dysfunctional family." Our parents didn't know they should have signed us all up for group therapy and anger management classes, and they also didn't know that the solution to their kids acting up was to have their actions diagnosed as a condition and then medicate us.

- Somehow we all survived bee stings without Benadryl.
- We used to be able to get an aspirin from the school nurse if we had a headache.
- We ate cupcakes, white bread and real butter, peanut butter and jam sandwiches, and drank sugar pop (you might have called it soda), but we weren't overweight because *we were always outside playing!*
- We would leave home in the morning and were allowed to be out playing all day, as long as we were back when the streetlights came on. No one was able to reach us all day. And we were OK.
- We would spend hours building our go-carts out of wood scraps and then ride down the hill, only to find out we forgot the brakes. After running into the bushes a few times, we learned to solve the problem.
- We did not have Playstations, Nintendos, X-Boxes; no video games at all, no 99-channel cable, no DVDs, no surround sound, no cell phones, no personal computers, no Internet or Internet chat rooms... we had friends and we went outside and found them!
- We fell out of trees, got cut, broke bones and teeth and there were no lawsuits from these accidents.
- We were given BB guns for our 10th birthdays, made up games with sticks and tennis balls and although we were told it would happen, we did not put out any eyes.
- We rode our bike or walked to a friend's house and knocked on the door or rang the bell, or just walked in and talked to them!
- Little League had tryouts and not everyone made the team. Those who didn't had to learn to deal with disappointment. Imagine that!
- The idea of a parent bailing us out if we broke the law was unheard of. They actually sided with the law!

- Not you or anyone you knew owned a purebred dog.
- A quarter was a decent allowance – but you only got it if you did your chores.
- All your male teachers wore neckties and female teachers had their hair done every day and wore high heels.
- When you pulled into a gas station, you got your windshield cleaned, oil checked, and gas pumped, without asking, all for free, every time. And you didn't pay for air, and, you got trading stamps, free glasses or Hot Wheels to boot.
- Laundry detergent had free glasses, dishes, or towels hidden inside the box.
- It was considered a great privilege to be taken out to dinner at a real restaurant with your parents.
- We would lie on our backs in the grass with our friends on lazy summer afternoons and said things like, "That cloud looks like a…"
- We could play baseball without adults to help us with the rules of the game.
- Stuff from the store came without safety caps and hermetic seals because no one had yet tried to poison a perfect stranger.
- When we were sent to the principal's office, it was nothing compared to the fate that awaited us at home.
- Our summers were filled with bike rides, baseball games in sandlots, Hula Hoops, bowling, visits to the pool, and playing Frisbee.
- Saturday morning cartoons were funny (and by today's standards, much too violent), but at least they weren't 30-minute commercials for action figures.
- "Oly-oly-oxen-free" made perfect sense.
- We would purposely spin around until we got so dizzy we fell down laughing and watched our world spin around and around. And then we'd do it all again.

- We put playing cards in the spokes of our stingrays to transform them into motorcycles.
- Car headlights dimmer switches were on the floor-board.
- We wore rubber bands wrapped around our pants legs for bicycles without chain guards.
- Wax Coke-shaped bottles with colored sugar water.
- Candy cigarettes.
- We got our soda pop from pop machines that dispensed bottles, and we had to open the top using the bottle opener built into the front of the machine.
- Most of the coffee shops and cafes had tableside jukeboxes.
- Milk was delivered to our homes in glass bottles with cardboard stoppers.
- Party lines and using the operator were just a normal part of using the telephone.
- We had tennis shoes called "smileys." They were black canvas with white toes and red, green or blue stripes around the front. They were similar to P.F. Flyers.
- Telephone numbers had word prefixes (Lincoln 2-xxxx).
- Peashooters or spit-wad shooters.
- We bought 45 RPM records of the latest top-40 hits.
- Metal ice trays with those levers that you had to pull up on to get the ice out – they were better at making ice shards than ice cubes.
- Mimeograph paper and the blue powder ink that got everywhere.
- Blue flashcubes for our mom's instamatic cameras.
- Pump-up BB guns. How many *thousands* of BBs did we all shoot?

- Drive-ins. They were great fun for the family but probably the worst way to try to actually watch a movie.
- Tinker-toys, Lincoln Logs, Erector sets and all those great toys that helped us build things using our hands and imagination.
- When we could feed the whole family at McDonald's for less than 10 bucks.
- 5 cent packs of baseball cards - with that awful pink slab of bubble gum.
- Penny candy.
- 35 cents a gallon gasoline.
- Jiffy Pop popcorn; Popcorn made in a pan on the stove with oil; there was no such thing as microwave popcorn – there was no such thing as a microwave.

Epilogue

This is nothing more than an opportunity for me to tell you that I'm finally done. To proclaim that after 3+ years of effort (working on again/off again; having a high level of inspiration vs. having an "I'll *never* finish" attitude; trying really hard to even think of something to write vs. madly scribbling down key words when ideas hit me so fast at the least convenient time (or in the most inconvenient places) I have finally crossed my last "t," dotted my last "i," and set my virtual "pen" down.

I'm not a writer. I never in my wildest dreams thought I would write a book. Ask my wife – I hardly even *read* books. She has a fairly extensive library of great books, my "library" consists of 95% comic books (*Calvin and Hobbes, The Far Side*, etc.) and is less than one shelf in a bookcase in our study. But something hit me when I began to realize that whenever my friends and I brought up these issues, or whenever one of these "Hey, look at that! Man, back when *I* was a kid…" thoughts ran through my mind, my ears perked up. I thought to myself, "If I was in a bookstore (hypothetically speaking here, of course) and I saw this book, I would probably pick it up and at least thumb through it. And – if I saw some of the things written in this book – I might even consider buying it. Maybe even pick one up for my friends who do read books on a regular basis who might get a kick out of it. I realized that the memories that came back to me always made me happy, maybe in a sort of melancholy way, but happy nonetheless. I knew then that if I felt that way, others might too.

I also know that I'm not the only person with fond memories of the '70s. There's a good chance that many books like this could be written because there's a whole generation of us who have had our own lifetime of experiences. Every one of those people – if they were crazy enough to try to fit writing into their already busy lives – would realize that they had some very special times growing up.

Maybe you're one of those people...

Maybe, if you were to pester your family and friends for their memories of your life growing up, you'd realize what a treasure your family really is to you. And maybe if you sifted through old boxes in your folks' attics, you'd realize what great times you had with simple things, and how much simpler life was when you were a kid. And maybe – just maybe – if you did all this, you might consider writing it all down so others might be inspired to do the same thing.

I did, and my life is richer for it.

Printed in the United States
140499LV00003BA/2/P